HURRY UP.

A GOOD SHOT.

A CORNER

HERE I AM

BACK THEN

BACK THEN

A PICTORIAL HISTORY OF AMERICANS AFIELD

To all the old-timers
who were, are and will be.

Published in the United States
by Willow Creek Press,
P.O. Box 300, Wautoma, WI 54982

ISBN O-932558-50-X

First edition; August 1989

014811. A GLIMPSE OF UPPER ST. REGIS LAKE

ACKNOWLEDGMENTS

PHOTO CREDITS: BIG GAME – Library of Congress, photographs 1, 2, 4, 5,6,7,8, 9, 11, 15, 16, 17, 18, 19, 20, 21, 22, 25, 26, 28, 34a, 34b, 34c, 34d, 37, 38, 40, 41, 42, 45, 46, 47, 48, 51, 52, 59, 60, 59b, 62, 63, 63; Colorado Historical Society, 3, 53, 54; M.V. Hall collection, New Mexico State Records & Archives, 10; Wyoming State Archives, Museums and Historical Department, 12, 23 , 55, 58; Oregon Historical Society, 13,57; California Historical Society Library, 14; Crawford County Museum, 29; State Historical Society of Wisconsin, 27, 30, 31, 32, 33 44, 49, 50; Vermont Historical Society, 35; State Historical Society of Iowa, 36; Minnesota Historical society, 39; Idaho Historical Society, 56; Oklahoma Historical Society 61. FISHING – Library of Congress, photographs 1, 2, 4,5, 6, 14, 15, 16, 17, 18, 19 ,20, 21, 23, 26, 28, 29, 31, 32, 33, 34, 36, 37, 39, 42, 43, 44; State Historical Society of Wisconsin, 3, Oregon Historical Society, 7, 8, 9; Minnesota Historical Society, 10, 38, 40; Colorado Historical Society, 11,13; Idaho Historical Society, 12, 21, 27, 30; Oklahoma Historical society, 22, 24; State Historical Society of Iowa, 25; Wyoming State Archives, Museums and Historical Department, 33a, 33b; Vermont Historical Society, 35; State Historical Society of Missouri, 41. FORESTS & UPLANDS – Library of Congress, photographs 1, 2, 3, 4, 5, 6, 10, 11, 13a, 15, 17, 18, 19, 20, 21, 22, 23, 25, 30, 31, 32, 33, 35a, 35b, 35c, 35d, 35e; South Dakota State Historical society, 7, 8, 9, 16; Minnesota Historical Society, 12; State Historical Society of Wisconsin, 13, 28, 29; Vermont Historical Society, 14; Oklahoma Historical Society, 25, 26, 27; Idaho Historical Society, 34. WATERFOWL – Library of Congress, photographs 1, 2, 3, 4, 5, 6, 8, 9, 10, 11, 12, 13, 14, 15, 16, 26, 29; Minnesota Historical Society, 7, 23; Nebraska State Historical Society, 17, 27; South Dakota State Historical Society, 18, 19, 20, 25; State Historical Society of Iowa, 21, 22, 28; State Historical Society of Wisconsin, 24, 30. TITLE PAGE; Wyoming State Archives, Museums and Historical Department.

FOREWORD

America's rich and colorful hunting and fishing history has been well chronicled in a wide assortment of literature since the days of European settlement. Indeed, much of our sporting heritage is preserved and passed on to us through the words of sportsmen of yesteryear. Often neglected, however but also offering unique insights into our past, is the photographic chronicle that complements, and occasionally contradicts, the written record of how Americans participated in outdoor sports. Providing some of those insights is the purpose of BACK THEN. The photographs assembled here encompass a period from the 1870s to the 1940s and represent only modest selections from the archives of the Library of Congress and museums and historical societies throughout the country. Theses photos were complied and edited by fellow sportsmen, not historical scholars, for BACK THEN does not assume to be a comprehensive academic presentation, but a warm, even sentimental, recollection of the less complicated America we shall never know again.

Illustrated here is an era when fish and game were more bountiful – and more abundantly harvested – than today. At the casual level, we are sometimes amused by the theatrical posing typical of staged photographs of the various periods, and sometimes vaguely resentful of the rapaciousness of those times and the large body counts of fish and game. At another level, however, we become witness to factual sporting history as each photograph thrusts the dim past suddenly and clearly before present vision, allowing the observer to interpret and reconstruct that history as it reveals itself through the photographic record.

Of course, we shall never really know how it felt to be on the short-grass prairie on an October day in 1912 when the tri-colored setter locked up on those sharptails; or feel the greenheart rod throb in our hand as a 10-pound steelhead raced for fast water, trailing our silk line behind it; or fully appreciate the hardships, dangers, or even the humor of the hunting and fishing camps or yore. Yet we can sense a wistful camaraderie with those kindred sportsmen who stare back at us from these pages and from that long-lost era. So, let's journey back the best we can, through the words and pictures presented here, in a book made with loving imprecision, a book intended to give us a better understanding of ourselves today through glimpses of who we were … back then.

The Editors
Willow Creek Press

9

CONTENTS

BIG GAME

A RECORD MOOS
HEAD 69 INCH
KILLED IN ALASKA
BY
DALL DE WEES
CAÑON CITY C
1897

2. "Perils of Frontier Life – A Fierce Encounter with a Giant of the Forest." Copyright 1905. Whether this staged stereoscopic scene was intended as high drama or comedy is unknown, although the hunter preparing to clobber the bear also seems to be stifling a smile.

BIG GAME

A MOOSE HUNT IN ALASKA

Cook's Inlet, Head of Kusiloff River

Moose Camp, Sept. 9, 1897

Consistent as I am with human nature, boys, I wanted one more moose and I don't believe you will say, "game hog," for you must remember that I am a long way from home and where these animals seem plenty and I am saving the skins and antlers to be mounted for my museum. Up to this time I could have killed two other moose with small heads (about 45 to 50 inches) and two cows and one calf moose, but I did not want them. After I secured my first bull it was then a good one or none. If you give this letter to our home paper and it should fall into the hands of some of the "would-be sportsmen," I will hear them yell "hog," but I should dread to see them have the opportunities for slaughter that I have been surrounded by on this trip.

The next day or two we looked up a better route through the timber to the lake and succeeded by following a well-worn bear trail which led in that direction. Mr. Berg still continued to pack my trophies to the lower camp and did not return that night, so I was alone in these far-away wilds some eighty miles from all

but one living man, and he was twelve miles away. As night came on I had a good fire going in front of the "lean to" and sat down on some fir boughs. Had you been with me I know how you would have enjoyed your pipe and tobacco, but as I don't use it I sat there long into the night gazing into the fire; yes, all alone, high up on the rolling timbered table lands at the head of Kusiloff River, and my friend alone down at the lake. With lightning rapidity I recalled all your faces and reminiscences of our grand old times in former years, when I lived in Troy, and we made our campfires on the Ausable, Manistee and Fife Lake, Michigan; camps on the Au Plain, Menomonee and Spread Eagle Lake, Wisconsin; Swan River and head waters of the Mississippi in Minnesota; Devil's Lake, Dakota; camps on Black and White River, Arkansas (where we had those turkey roasts and duck bakes in our "clay dutch oven;") then, dear Jim, the camps on Savogle and Marinuchi in New Brunswick; camps in Wyoming, Utah, Montana, Mexico and all the streams that head in the big game country of our Colorado from North Park south to the head of the Bear, Williams, both forks of the White, the Grand, Eagle, Piney, Gunnison and southward to the San Juan. In the burning embers of my

---

1. "A record 60-inch moose head, killed in Alaska by Dall DeWeese, Canon City, Col., 1887." Mr DeWeese proudly donned his bush garb for this studio photo. The story of this hunt begins this chapter.

3

3. An elk camp in the White River area of Colorado. Note the hunting hounds at rest.

4. "Early morning breakfast – before beginning the hunt – head of Horse Creek, Montana." Copyright 1906.

5. "A Night in the bed of Grapevine Creek, Grand Canyon of Arizona." Copyright 1903.

6. A hunting packtrain in the Idaho foothills, circa 1905. Otto M. Johnson photo.

4

5

6

7

8

9

7. "Elk hunting in the mountain woods of N.W. Wyoming, U.S.A." Copyright 1904.

8. The boys bring out the heavy artillery.

9. "A Lucky Shot," ca. 1906, on a mountain goat.

campfire, I could in my fancy see all your faces, and how gratifying to know that those of you who were with me were true sportsmen and never a thing occurred to mar the pleasure of our outing, for the good and bad side of a man or woman will be revealed in camp. How I wished you all with me that night and tonight for I am having too much sport on this trip to enjoy it alone.

As my fire burned low I rolled up my blankets and crawled under the "lean to" upon a caribou skin on some spruce feathers, and then with a thought of the dear ones at home, what tomorrow's luck would be, and with weary body I was soon in dreamland. Daylight next morning found me preparing a hurried breakfast of moose steak, boiled rice, tor-te-os (fry pan bread) and tea. I ate heartily, for I intended to make in a new direction that day. I had a birch horn with me and had tried the "call" one evening for three hours without success and thought I would take it with me this morning. About 7 I tried the "call" more out of curiosity than otherwise; first, the "short call," then the "long call," and repeated several times. An hour passed and

finally my patience was rewarded by a light crackling behind me. I listened – then a thud between the alders. I then made a "low call" and soon his mooseship waded through the patch of alders and stood in open ground (other than the tall grass) not more than sixty yards from me. Oh, for a camera. He would swing his head to and fro, sniffing the air; then lowering it with muzzle extended stood silently working his ears forward, then back. I had detected a slight puff of air and noticed it to be in his favor. Suddenly he raised his head high and sniffed loudly and slowly swung around and made for the low timber; not rapidly, but simply as if he had made a mistake. He was a big brute but his antlers were much inferior to those I had. My curiosity being satisfied, I again moved cautiously along much amused; how plainly I can recall his every move, and I want to tell you I didn't like that kind of moose hunting. I was dressed for "still hunting," and as I moved silently along how little I dreamed that I would be rewarded in not killing this last animal by having in my path a much better specimen of moose than I had yet seen.

10. *Stand hunting in the mountains of Arizona.*

About 10, while still hunting through rolling ground with patches of spruce and tall grass, I sighted a cow lying down within eighty yards. I looked carefully, knowing the velvet was now off and a bull might be near, and after crawling a rod or so I saw the wide white blade of a bull between the trees close to the edge of the timber. I put my glasses on him to look at his horns but it seems he had sniffed me and a startled glance showed his big horns. The cow ran to my left – the bull to my right, quartering and a little down hill. My first ball caught him in the short ribs on the right side and stopped at the skin in front of the left shoulder; he stopped and swung around broadside. I sent another clean through him. He headed off again and I pitched another one into him. He again stopped broadside and coughed hard and when his great sides would heave I saw the blood spout from the wounds. I knew he was done for, and while he stood there with lowered head I ran around and below him as I had heard a terrible rolling through the tall grass (four feet high) below him, and thought it must be a bear making off. I could see

nothing and returned to the moose expecting to find him down and dead; but imagine my surprise when on coming up a little raise I found myself within thirty yards of that great brute on his feet and coming toward me with his head lowered, shaking those massive antlers. I can't tell how I did it but as I afterwards found I sent a ball at his head which caught him in the brisket. Still he came and my next ball was better aimed and struck between the eyes. That stopped him and he sank down upon his limbs but did not roll over. Boys, I am frank to acknowledge that I was startled. I am cold yet – never have I had even a grizzly give me such a feeling. As he came through that tall grass breathing the blood and tossing those wicked antlers, truly he looked like an old McCormick self-binder.

I was carrying my new Mannlicher that day and right there saw an advantage in smokeless powder as well as once more before the day closed. However, I have used the Winchester for twenty-four years; in fact, my first hunt for deer in Henry County, O., when but 16 years old, was with the old rimfire Henry rifle and when the

19

King's model of 73 Winchester came out, I got that and have used all models since and had them made specially to fit me. I have now in camp my special made 40-70-330 metal patched soft-nose, black powder 86 model Winchester, which I have used for the past four years. I brought both my guns on this hunt for fear something might go wrong with one or the other. Boys, you wanted me to report on this Mannlicher and I must say that it is the most deadly gun I ever carried. Its great velocity of 2000 feet per second and its extreme flat trajectory makes it very desirable for long range shooting. At three to four hundred yards if held on the game the ball is into it almost the instant you touch the trigger. I was using the metal patch soft nose which will mushroom on flesh and the patch seems to be slightly cut with the lands of the barrel when fired and expands like a buzz-saw. The sheep when struck drop as limp as a rag, and the moose no matter in what part of the body he was struck seemed paralyzed from the first shot. Again, the gun is very light, which is a great advantage when you pack your loads on your back. You know I am not an agent for the Mannlicher works, but let honor fall where it is due. There is, however, an objection to the close range between sights, for you must hold very carefully or you miss. This can be remedied by a peep on the rear of the hammer. I don't think they have any of these small calibers quite perfected; a few years more experiment will doubtless make a great improvement in them.

Well, there I stood beside my giant moose, without a camera or a friend with me to admire my prize. Oh, what a carcass. I had my steel tape with me and commenced his measurements and now give them to you as I put them down in my diary. Of course, the first measurement was the spread of his antlers which is sixty-nine inches; length of beam, forty-eight inches; palmations fifteen inches; circumference of beam burr at head fourteen and one-half inches; circumference of beams at smallest place ten inches; antlers have thirty-two points. His great body measured sixteen feet four inches from lip to point of rear hoof; seven feet eight inches from front hoof to top of withers; girted eight feet nine inches, six feet seven inches around the neck at shoulders; thirty-three and one-half inches from tip to tip of ears; ears seven inches wide and forty-four inches around the lips of the open mouth. What a match he will be when mounted for my big elk. Boys, I know that I hew close enough to the line of "true sportsmanship" not to be overcome by selfishness and will say that all points considered, size, massiveness, etc., I believe I have a world beater; but be this as it may I will be satisfied when I get it packed out and home. Some hunters saw the heads through the skull and then when being mounted by some they are given more spread; I know of a moose head whose spread was eight inches more when mounted than it was before it was sawed apart and an elk head that is seventeen inches more than it was naturally. I haven't a sawed head in my collection and would not take one as a gift for mounting. This method doesn't belong to true sportsmanship, and it makes the animal look very unnatural. They say it was necessary to saw them apart to get them out of the terrible country. I say that big game animal doesn't exist in such a country that makes it impossible to get the antlers out whole. I don't believe there has been game killed in a worse country of access than this. For many miles there is a mass of down timber, criss-crossed and

11. A handsomely composed 1903 stereoscopic photo – "A dandy shot, Jim, see where the bullet blazed him."

12. Packing elk out of the Wyoming high country on travois.

13. "On Germantown Trail (Idaho) with pack horses."

12

13

covered with slippery moss, and intergrown with tall grass and bushes; then canyons and ice cold streams to cross, but I intend to take those antlers down and out without sawing them if it takes all winter.

But back to the moose. It took me till 1 p.m. to dress him and I then started towards camp in the rain with the neck skin which was all I could carry, and content in mind that Alaska is the home of the largest moose in the world, and why not when this country affords such wonderful growth for food, and he lives to get age, which he must have to grow large horns; then his healthy condition does the rest.

About 3 in the afternoon, drenched, tired and hungry I was at the edge of the heavy spruce and thick willows six to ten feet in height and heard a cracking near me – thought 'twas a moose – then saw the willows shake near me, and stepping upon a rotten log and looking about, there, within twenty-five feet, on his hind legs, looking at me over the willows, stood one of those fighting Alaskan grizzlies. I had this neck skin of moose, shot pouch fashion, over my neck with left arm free; but in an instant I cocked my Mannlicher while bringing it in position and plugged him through the neck just under the head. He dropped and I stepped from the log that I could see better under the willows and sent another ball through his shoulders while he was roaring and fighting the willows and ground. I used lead and gave him another through the neck which settled him. I still kept the neck skin on, thinking to use it for a shield if he charged me. He had evidently scented the skin and was coming right after it. This was some sport. He is a monster, has claws four inches long, head twenty-two inches from nose to ears, measures ten feet seven inches stretch; foot eight by twelve inches and had a good coat of hair.

It took me till dark to skin him out and after it was off I could not lift it. I dragged it over the willows and left it and got in camp after dark thinking Alaska had bears of uncomfortable size and numbers for night travelling while alone.

As I approached camp I gave my usual shrill whistle and was answered by Mr. Berg through his gun barrel. Boys, how glad I was to hear it and when he came out to meet me, gave a hearty hand shake and then relieved me of my heavy load. As I neared the fire how appetizing was the smell of his good supper already prepared, and I might add that my day's work without food had something to do with my appetite.

I was drenched to the skin and after a partial change of footwear we were soon drying, eating and talking of my "red letter day" which pleased my big hardy companion seemingly as much as myself; yet we knew that we had both taken great risks in being alone in these wilds.

This ended my hunt in Alaska. I have killed two specimens hard to duplicate, and of the class of animals of which I have had such a desire to add to my collection. I am more than pleased and wish all my hunting friends were here now, to take a look and a shake. Mr. Berg says they are more massive and heavier than the record head he killed two years ago which was mentioned in *Forest and Stream* of March 6th, 1897.

It has been raining and snowing all day. We will now pack everything down to the lake and I will care for my heads and skins and work homeward as fast as possible, for truly I feel that I am well paid for my long and tiresome journey of 8,000 miles, round trip, on land and sea. I am compelled to travel 185 miles from here on foot and log canoe to reach the steamboat landing. It is now too dark to write and will finish at lower camp. We will make supper of moose steak, boiled rice, wild red currant sauce and tea.

Dall DeWeese in OUTDOOR LIFE, January, 1898

A HUNT IN THE WOODS OF NORTHERN MICHIGAN

At intervals along both banks of the river are high bluffs, where the plain ends in a precipitous descent to the river. These bluffs, many of them, have been used by the lumbermen as rollways (as they are called); logs and timber are here thrown into the river from a height of fifty to seventy feet. At a point nearest to our camp is situated two such bluffs separated by a deep ravine.

This spot is on the outer circle of a grand sweep or bend in the river, and with me is a favorite place. From here you overlook the opposite shore which, rising gradually from the water, is densely wooded with that most somber and picturesque of all trees, the white cedar; the dark green of the balsams and other kindred firs stretching away in grand panoramic beauty to the distant hills. The wild sweep of the beautiful river, the whole scene as looked down on from the bluffs, is a picture worthy the pencil of a Bierstadt or a Landseer.

---

14. "Taking aim," albumen print, date unknown.

15. "At Headquarters – Our Christmas Hunt," 1897. Note skis propped against the cabin roof.

14

15

16

17

18

19

20

21

22

16 - 21. *Preceding spread: To fill time in camp, the boys staged a little northwoods moose rodeo, circa 1912.*

22. *"Come on boys, we've got him – the lord of the forest slain,"* 1906. *Stereoscopic photographers went to great lengths to create interesting photos. The blaze on the tree was likely made to ensure the dead moose could be found again after the men left the scene to fetch cumbersome photo equipment.*

23. *Moose hunting in Wyoming. Date unknown, but circa 1930-35.*

24. *"Glory Enough for One Day,"* 1899, *featuring the oft-used scene of hunters examining the bullet's point of entry. Note the woolen leggings of hunters on left.*

23

24

25. "The Call of the Wild," 1907; a classic birch bark moose call echoes through the cedars.

Not caring to hunt one morning, I had gone to the place described for an hour's enjoyment of the free, wild spot. The hounds were out, and the Doctor was on the watch some forty rods above where I sat. Very soon in the Doctor's direction I heard the quick sharp cry of a dog running on close scent. A moment later and a noble buck took the water within reach of the Doctor's rifle; one, two, and a third shot from the Winchester and the deer was across and into the woods on the other side. Had I the pen of "the wizard of the north," the power in fitting words to tell how "twice that day from shore to shore the gallant stag swam stoutly o'er," to enable the reader to take in the whole wild picture as I saw it, I should be amply paid for the telling. Five minutes had not elapsed when the hound in pursuit was at the bank. Plunging in and swimming bravely across, he picked up the scent.

Two or three cries from the dog told that the game was found; back rushed the deer into the water, but alas, poor hunted quarry, with a disabled shoulder. He had only reached the middle of the stream when he was met by another foe. This was no other than a large Newfoundland belonging to Curtis (grand old Carlo, a terror to the bears of the Sable). Both dogs were soon in reach of the buck, and all in the rapid stream came sweeping down in my direction. The brave deer battled nobly for his life, tearing the dogs loose with a blow from his horns whenever they seized him about the head.

Not a cry from the gallant stag. Not a bleat of terror. So the battle went on as dogs and deer drifted past me at

my feet and soon were lost to view by a bend in the river. Finally, by the help of Curtis in the canoe, the noble game was slain and brought to shore. My diagnosis of the case accuses the Doctor of mal-practice; he should have shot him in the head and let him die a warrior's death.

The battle above described had barely drifted out of site, when hearing the cry of hounds, and turning my eyes in the direction of the bluff below me, I listened for a minute and saw a beautiful doe, with one wild grand leap, throw herself from the brow of the precipice. Graceful in her flight as a bird on the wing, she landed safely on the sand some forty feet below. I looked, expecting to see her fall or stumble; but no, without a halt, on she went, and soon all that could be seen of her was her beautiful head floating away in the rapid stream.

This had hardly transpired when, looking in the Doctor's direction – he still remaining at his post – I saw swimming down towards him another of these fairies of the woods. One sharp crack of the rifle, one short struggle, and she floated past with a cruel bullet through her brain.

What with the grand wild view that lay before me, the battle at my feet, the death of the noble game – the hour thus spent has left an impression that cannot be forgotten or effaced...

S.
from "The Chicago Field," 1877

26

27

26. *A gorgeous cedar-stripped Adirondack guide boat complete with hunters, whitetail buck and hunting hounds.*

27. *Hauling a buck out of the Wisconsin northwoods, circa 1905. In the crowded woods of today, such mode of transportation would be suicidal.*

28. *"Hunting in the Adirondacks," circa 1912; a nicely staged and composed photograph.*

28

A Hunter Lost in Wyoming Snow Storm

Editor, Outdoor Life: – I was expecting to be able to write a story for you again this year, but my expectations fell very hard. I was unable to get away last fall, but my hunting partner, Cy Allen, the man who was with me last fall, left here October 2nd for the same place in Jackson Hole in which we hunted last fall. On November 5th he started up Cub Creek, south and east of Buffalo Fork, and this was the last time he was ever seen. When he did not show up in two or three days a search was made for him. It started snowing the morning he left camp and already there was ten inches of snow, and it didn't quit for nineteen days longer.

After he was gone eleven days his dog came to a ranger's cabin down along Long Creek and in all probability Mr. Allen was in the Long Creek country. This would make him thirty or thirty-five miles from his camp, and also east of Brooks' Lake, when the dog left him.

Bert Rowels has been hunting for him ever since he was lost, but without avail. There are no hopes now and the chances are against him if his body is ever found. He leaves a wife and two babies; also a mother and a brother. He was a very close friend of mine, and being an ardent lover of hunting and fishing, also one of the party, with me a year ago, I thought probably you would be interested. If this letter would reach the eye of any brother sportsman going into that part of the country I hope they will keep an eye open for Mr. Allen's body. He is somewhere between Cub Creek, north of Black Rock, and Long Creek, east of Brooks' Lake.

This accident has somewhat broken up my hunting this last fall.

W. B. Millett, Wyoming
from OUTDOOR LIFE, 1911

29

30

29, 30, 31. Railroad trains were for many years the primary mode of hunter transport into the North. Depots became staging areas for hunters who were then shuttled by buckboard or automobile to their hunting camps. These photos of northern Michigan and Wisconsin depots depict the end of the hunt as hunters await to entrain with their trophies.

NORTHERN LIVES

Most of us who run and read do not require proof to know that the way of the musher is hard. The long Alaska winters alone, with none of the accompanying hardships, would ensure that. Probably in no other country on the globe does the prospector and trapper encounter such heart-rending obstacles as in Alaska. A large number of these men whom you meet in that country – those whose lives are spent in the open – are going to get away from it "next fall." They need a larger stake, or they wish to finish just one task; then they intend to hike to the "outside" – as the States is called. But only a small percentage of those rosy dreams ever are realized, for before they know it something has happened that makes their exit from that land less likely than ever before. A bad fall in the glaciers, or a frozen and amputated foot, or hands, nose or ears may have been disfigured from freezing, with the result that they feel that they "belong" very well where they are.

A large number of the men of the Arctic wouldn't live anywhere else. They seem to have been seized with the lure of the Northland – which is there, all right, for those who like it, just as you find men who get fascinated with the desert, and who can't give it up – and once this spell is upon them, you might as well try to induce Mt. Shishaldin to shift positions as attempt to jar them loose from their enthrallment.

We are indebted to A. M. Bailey (an Alaskan of some years' experience) for complete detailed diaries kept by

31

"Sourdoughs" previous to their respective deaths in different localities of Alaska. In each of these cases they were alone and so far from civilization that, in their terribly weakened condition [could not] reach assistance....

Note: – This is a correct copy of the diary left by one V. Swanson, known as the "Wildman of Dry Bay," whose body was found on the 18th of August, 1918, by Hardy Trefger and Fred Zastrow, trappers from Dry Bay:

1917

Oct. 28 – Winter has come. Strong wind, two feet of snow.

Nov. 4 – Shot one lynx.

6 – Made one pair of bearskin pants.

8 – Sugar is all gone.

13 – Made two pair of moccasins.

18 – Finished one fur coat of bear, wolf and lynx.

21 – Finished one sleeping bag of bear, goat, blankets and canvas. Rain for several days.

22 – Left eye bothers me. Shot one goat.

26 – Shot one lynx while eating breakfast.

27 – Made one pair of bearpaw snowshoes.

Dec. 1 – Getting bad. Cold for several days, river still open.

4 – River raised six feet in twenty-four hours.

6 – Slush stiffening slowly, making ice.

7 – The wind is so strong that you can't stand upright. Snow getting deeper now.

15 – Very cold and strong wind, impossible to be out without skin clothes.

19 – Snowing, but still very cold. Can't travel. Very little grub; snow too deep and soft for hunting goats. Stomach balking at straight meat, especially lynx.

21 – Shot a goat from the river.

25 – Very cold. A good Christmas dinner. Snow getting hard.

26 – Broke through the ice. Skin clothes saved the day.

31 – Finished new roof on the house. One month cold weather straight. Stomach getting worse.

32

33

32. *Elaborately posed whitetails (central Wisconsin, 1908), ears tagged and ready for railroad shipment home.*

33. *The meat pole of this northern Wisconsin deer camp, circa 1900, hangs heavy. The dead, juvenile bald eagle and the mounted fawn are, by today's standards, sad testament to unsportsmanlike, indiscriminate shooting.*

32

34 a

34 b

34 a through d. Stereoscopic photographs, which appeared three-dimensional through the viewer, were extremely popular forms of entertainment through the late 1800s and early 1900s. Exotic, foreign lands and the romance-filled American frontier were of particular interest to the public. Not content with mere landscapes, photographers in this competitive field often went to great lengths to reconstruct or contrive action scenes, as typified here.

a. "He is our Meat (Antelope)"

b. "A double kill in the early morning twilight. Indian Territory, U.S.A.," 1901.

c. "A Struggle with Bruin in the Wild of Oregon"

d. "Bear Shooting on the Frontier," 1905.

34 c

34 d

Jan. 8 – River open as far as can be seen. Health very poor.

12 – Lynx moving down river one or two a night; no chance to catch them.

15 – Goats moving out of reach. Using canoe on the river.

16 – One lynx. Weather getting mild.

20 – Rain today.

22 – One lynx.

28 – One goat; been cold for a few days.

Feb. 1 – Cold weather nearly all month of January. Lynx robbed my meat cache up the river. Salt and tea once a day. Gradually getting weaker.

5 – Colder weather; feeling very bad. Just able to take care of myself.

10 – Milder weather, feeling very bad. Heavy fall of snow.

15 – Good weather continues; feeling some better.

24 – More snow. Living on dry meat and tallow.

26 – Shot one goat from the river.

Mar. 2 – Shot one goat.

11 – Starting for Dry Bay, believing the river open. Out about one hour, struck the ice; can't go either way; too weak to haul the canoe. Snow soft; no game here.

25 – Trying to get to the house. River is frozen in places and rising. The sleigh now only three miles from there, but open river and perpendicular cliffs keep me from getting any farther. At present cannot find anything to eat here. Eyes are getting bad.

28 – Eyes can't stand the sun at all. Finest kind of weather.

Apr. 1 – Got to the house with what I could carry. Wolverines had been there eating my skins, robes and moccasins, old meat and also my goat skin door. They tried to run me last night; came through the stovepipe hole, showing fight. Heavy fall of snow. Canoe and some traps down river about five miles close to Indian grave mark. Camp about half-ways.

3 – Still snowing. Cooking my last grub; no salt; no tea.

4 – Shot one goat, using all but three of my shells. Can't see the sight at all.

7 – Wolverines working on camp below, carrying away my things. Ate part of my bearskin pants.

Packed the old .30-30 out into the brush. Eyes are getting worse again; don't even stand the snow.

10 – Wolverines ate my bedding and one snowshoe. In the tent – getting shaky in the legs. A five-mile walk a big day's work.

12 – Seen a fox track today. Birds are coming, too. Fine weather.

15 – The no-salt diet hitting me pretty hard. Eyes are getting worse; in the bunk most of the time.

17 – Rain yesterday and today.

20 – Finest weather continues again; cooking the last grub; got to stay in the bunk most of the time; my legs won't carry me very far.

My eyes useless for hunting; the rest of my body also useless. I believe my time has come. My belongings – everything I got – I give to Jos. Pellerine of Dry Bay; if not alive to Paul Swartzkopf, Alesk River. April 22, 1918.

(signed)   V. Swanson

This is the statement of a man found dead in his cabin by Barry Trefgar and myself on the 18th day of August, 1918.

(signed)   Fred Zastrow.

OUTDOOR LIFE, August, 1923

GENERAL CUSTER'S BUFFALO HUNT

Here I will refer to an incident entirely personal, which came very near costing me my life. When leaving our camp that morning I felt satisfied that the Indians, having traveled at least a portion of the night, were then many miles in advance of us, and there was neither danger nor probability of encountering any of them near the column. We were then in a magnificent game country, buffalo, antelope, and smaller game being in abundance on all sides of us. Although an ardent sportsman, I had never hunted the buffalo up to this time; consequently I was exceedingly desirous of tasting of its excitement. I had several fine English greyhounds, whose speed I was anxious to test with that of the antelope, said to be – which I believe – the fleetest of animals.

I was mounted on a fine large thoroughbred horse. Taking with me but one man, the chief bugler, and calling my dogs around me, I galloped ahead of the

35. The story belonging to this Vermont photograph is lost to history, but the clues of the axe and the timid dog forced to pose beside the bear give rise to the imagination. Perhaps the story went something like – "A hibernating bear, awakened by the spring thaw, hungrily grazed on fallen apples. Alerted to bruin by a barking dalmatian, the farmer fetched his axe and..."

36. *All decked out in their fancy hunting attire, Winchesters at their sides and hounds at their feet, this pair of Iowa hunters pose in the studio before their big game trip to the wilds of Minnesota, circa 1900.*

37-38. *Stereo photo of Alexander Cromwell, his dog, and the "enormous panther" shot in Barnard, Vermont, 1881. "He was shot at a distance of about one rod only," reads the text on the back of the photo, "and with a shotgun at first, and afterwards with a rifle. His movements were so noiseless that Mr. Cromwell found himself in this dangerous proximity before he was aware of it, and it was only by great coolness and daring that he severely wounded the animal and perhaps saved his life."*

Photograph of the Panther killed at Barnard, Vermont, Nov. 24, 1881, by Mr. Alexander Crowell, showing Mr. Crowell with his gun and his dog that attacked the Panther before he was shot.

This enormous Panther was shot in Barnard, Vermont, on November 24, 1881, by Alexander Crowell. He is the largest Panther of which history makes any record. He measures from the nose to the tip of the tail 7 feet, girths 3 feet and 8 inches, the circumference of his forearm is 22 inches, height 3 feet 8 inches, size of forehead 2 feet 9 inches and his weight when shot was 182 pounds.

In South America this animal is known as the Puma, or lion, and it is believed to be identical with the California lion, so called. In Vermont it has always been called by many a Catamount, but its true designation is the North American Panther, and this is the finest specimen ever exhibited. He was shot by Mr. Crowell at a distance of about one rod only, and with a shot gun at first, and afterwards with a rifle. His movements were so noiseless that Mr. Crowell found himself in this dangerous proximity before he was aware of it, and it was only by great coolness and daring that he severely wounded the animal and perhaps saved his own life.

This noble specimen of a very rare wild beast is now on exhibition throughout the country, and none, who can, should fail to improve the opportunity to see it.

G. R. SAFFORD, Proprietor.

column as soon as it was daylight for the purpose of having a chase after some antelope which could be seen grazing nearly two miles distant. That such a course was rashly imprudent I am ready to admit. A stirring gallop of a few minutes brought me near enough to the antelope, of which there were a dozen or more, to enable the dogs to catch sight of them.

The chase began, the antelope running in a direction which took us away from the command. By availing myself of the turns in the course, I was able to keep well in view of the exciting chase, until it was evident that the antelope were in no danger of being caught by the dogs, which latter had become blown for want of proper exercise. I succeeded in calling them off and was about to set out on my return to the column. The horse of the chief bugler, being a common-bred animal, failed early in the race, and his rider wisely concluded to regain the command, so I was alone.

How far I had traveled from the troops I was trying to determine when I discovered a large, dark-looking animal grazing nearly a mile distant. As yet I had never seen a wild buffalo, but I at once recognized this as not only a buffalo, but a very large one. Here was my opportunity. A ravine nearby would enable me to approach unseen until almost within pistol range of my game. Calling my dogs to follow me, I slowly pursued the course of the ravine, giving my horse opportunity to gather himself for the second run.

When I emerged from the ravine I was still several hundred yards from the buffalo, which almost instantly discovered me, and set off as fast as his legs could carry him. Had my horse been fresh, the race would have been a short one, but the preceding long run had not been without effect. How long or how fast we flew in pursuit, the intense excitement of the chase prevented me from knowing. I only knew that even the greyhounds were left behind, until finally my good steed placed himself and me close alongside the game. It may be because this was the first I had seen, but surely of the hundreds of thousands of buffaloes which I have since seen, none have corresponded with him in size and lofty grandeur.

My horse was above the average size, yet the buffalo towered even above him. I had carried my revolver in my hand from the moment the race began. Repeatedly could I have placed the muzzle against the shaggy body of the huge beast, by whose side I fairly yelled with wild excitement and delight, yet each time would I withdraw the weapon, as if to prolong the enjoyment of the race. It was a race for life or death, yet how different the award

from what could be imagined. Still we sped over the springy turf, the high breeding and mettle of my horse being plainly visible over that of the huge beast that struggled by his side. Mile after mile was traversed in this way, until the rate and distance began to tell perceptibly on the bison, whose protruding tongue and labored breathing plainly betrayed his distress. Determined to end the chase and bring down my game, I again placed the muzzle of the revolver close to the body of the buffalo, when, as if divining my intention and feeling his inability to escape by flight, he suddenly determined to fight, and at once wheeled, as only a buffalo can, to gore my horse.

So sudden was his movement, and so sudden was the corresponding veering of my horse to avoid the attack, that to retain my control over him I hastily brought up my pistol hand to the assistance of the other. Unfortunately, as I did so, my finger in the excitement of the occasion, pressed the trigger, discharged the pistol, and sent the fatal ball into the very brain of the noble animal I rode. Running at full speed, he fell dead in the course of his leap. Quick as thought I disengaged myself from the stirrups and found myself whirling through the air over and beyond the head of my horse.

My only thought, as I was describing this trajectory, and my first thought on reaching *terra firma*, was, "What will the buffalo do with me?" Although at first inclined to rush upon me, my strange procedure seemed to astonish him. Either that or pity for the utter helplessness of my condition inclined him to alter his course and leave me alone to my own bitter reflections.

In a moment the danger into which I had unluckily brought myself stood out in bold relief before me. Under ordinary circumstances the death of my horse would have been serious enough. I was strongly attached to him; had ridden him in battle during a portion of the late war; yet now his death, except in its consequences, was scarcely thought of. Here I was, alone in the heart of Indian country, with warlike Indians known to be in the vicinity. I was not familiar with the country. How far I had traveled, or in what direction from the column, I was at a loss to know. In the excitement of the chase I had lost all reckoning. Indians were liable to pounce upon me at any moment. My command would not note my absence probably for hours.

Two of my dogs overtook me, and with mute glances first at the dead steed, then at me, seemed to enquire the cause of this strange condition of affairs. Their instinct appeared to tell them that we were in misfortune. While I was deliberating what to do, the

---

39. Four Minnesota hunters posed, circa 1880, in the studio with their dogs and four bobcats.

40

41

40. *Adirondack deer hunters, 1888, pose in the light of a campfire (enhanced by crude photo retouching).*

41. *A 1903 stereograph – "Hanging Deer – 'Now, Guide, a Moose before Nightfall.' " The guide's reply to his arrogant client is not recorded.*

42. This 1903 stereo, obviously posed, illustrates the various chores required to keep a camp running smoothly. "Characteristic camp scene – preparing for supper and the night," reads the caption printed on the stereo.

43. By contrast, this more candid and less cozy scene of an Adirondacks deer camp under a dusting of fresh snow smacks of a reality rarely depicted in photographs of the era.

42

43

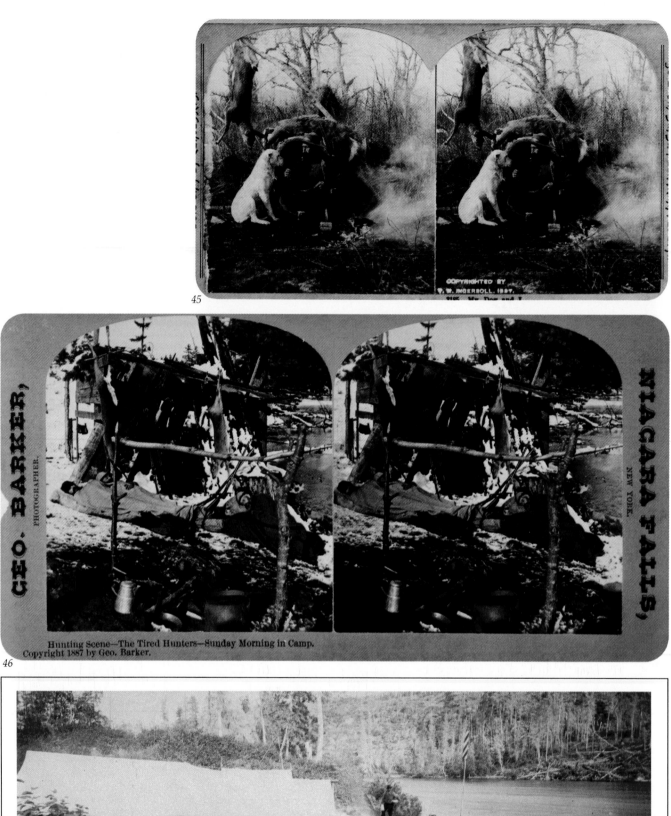

45

GEO. BARKER,
PHOTOGRAPHER.

NIAGARA FALLS,
NEW YORK.

Hunting Scene—The Tired Hunters—Sunday Morning in Camp.
Copyright 1887 by Geo. Barker.

46

47

44. *Preceding spread: A Taylor County, Wisconsin, deer camp of 1904. This pleasing photograph also shows unaffected detail, including a bootless hunter warming his feet, another camp member with boots unlaced, beer bottles on the table, and a mirror tacked to a tree.*

45. *A primitive slab-sided shelter provided room enough for gear but not the hunters in this 1887 camp.*

46. *This enterprising hunter and his dog called a hollow log home while in the bush in the autumn of 1897.*

47. *A relatively luxurious camp, proudly flying Old Glory, along the Nipigon River, in the spring of 1887. Note the brace of trout (lake-run rainbows?) held by angler at far left. An Indian guide, holding his canoe pole, sits before the stretched bearskin.*

48. *"Deer hunters camp in the Northwest," circa 1885. All three hunters are holding muzzle-loaders, and the hunters at left and right are wearing powder horns.*

49. *A huge, northern Wisconsin buck on the meat pole, 1904.*

50. *The humble interior of a deer hunting cabin of about 1893.*

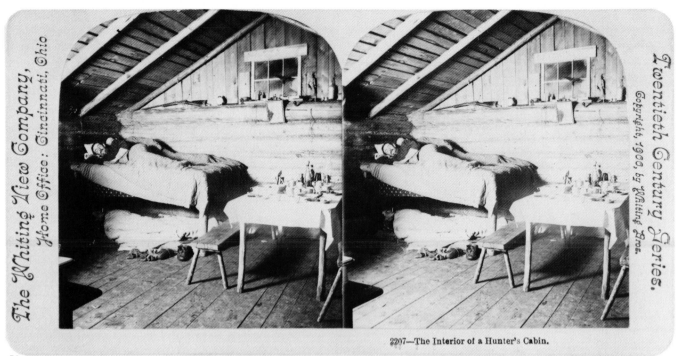

2207—The Interior of a Hunter's Cabin.

51

51. "The Interior of a Hunter's Cabin," 1900 – this one a bit tidier that the previous.

52. A card game in an Adirondack hunting camp, 1888.

---

dogs became uneasy, whined piteously, and seemed eager to leave the spot. In this desire I sympathized with them, but whither should I go? I observed that their eyes were generally turned in one particular direction; this I accepted as my cue, and with one parting look at my horse, and grasping a revolver in each hand, I set out on my uncertain journey.

As long as the body of my horse was visible above the horizon, I kept referring to it as my guiding point, and in this way contrived to preserve my direction. This resource soon failed me, and I then had recourse to weeds, buffalo skulls, or any two objects I could find on my line of march. Constantly my eyes kept scanning the horizon, each moment expecting, and with reason too, to find myself discovered by Indians.

I had traveled in this manner what seemed to me about three or four miles when far ahead in the distance I saw a column of dust rising. A hasty examination soon convinced me that the dust was produced by two or three causes; white men, Indians, or buffalo. Two to one in my favor at any rate. Selecting a ravine where I could crawl away undiscovered should the approaching body prove to be Indians, I called my dogs to my side and concealed myself as well as I could to await developments.

The object of my anxious solicitude was still several miles distant. Whatever it was, it was approaching in my direction, as was plainly discernible from the increasing columns of dust. Fortunately I had my field-glasses slung across my shoulder, and, if Indians, I could discover them before they could possibly discover me. Soon I was able to see the heads of mounted men running in irregular order. This discovery shut out the probability of their being buffaloes, and simplified the question to white men or Indians. Never during the war did I scan an enemy's battery or approaching column with half the anxious care with which I watched the party then approaching me.

For a long time nothing satisfactory could be determined, until my eye caught sight of an object which, high above the heads of the approaching riders, told me in unmistakable terms that friends were approaching. It was the cavalry guidon, and never was the sight of the stars and stripes more welcome. My comrades were greatly surprised to find me seated on the ground alone and without my horse. A few words explained all. A detachment of my men, following my direction, found my horse and returned with the saddle and other equipments. Another horse, and Richard was himself again, plus a little valuable experience and minus a valuable horse.

– from My Life on the Plains
by General George Armstrong Custer

54

55

53. Preceding spread: "Six day's hunt near Sringville, Colorado."

54. Mountain lion hunting camp near the North Rim, Grand Canyon, Arizona, about 1900.

55. "Mrs. Smith and wildcat killed near Glenrock, Wyoming."

56-57. Idaho lion hunters, circa 1898.

56

57

57 b

BUFFALO HUNTING IN WESTERN TEXAS

There is nothing here to gaze on save a few adobe and picket houses, corrals, and immense stacks of buffalo hides. The post, situated on a hill a quarter of a mile south, is almost depopulated, there being but one company of negro soldiers inhabiting it. F.E. Conrad's storeroom near the post, is the most extensive establishment in the place. It is here that the hunters procure their supplies and deliver most of the hides brought in. Yesterday Mr. Conrad's sales amounted to near $4,000, about $2,500 of which consisted of guns and ammunition. There are now said to be 1,500 hunters on the range, and most all of this number receive their supplies from this point, consequently the propriety of keeping such large stocks of ammunition and provisions. From Mr. Garrison I learn that he has en route from the prairies twelve hundred hides. He is also engaged in putting up meat, which he intends canvassing and shipping North. Men just in from the west report the buffaloes going southwest. They are now in the vicinity of Colorado Post on the Colorado River. – *Fort Worth Democrat*

from THE CHICAGO FIELD, 1877

WHAT HE SHOT

"What is the name of that species I just shot?" inquired the amateur hunter.

"Says his name is Smith, sir," answered the guide, who had been investigating.

– OUTDOOR LIFE, circa 1911

JACK RABBITS WITH ANTLERS
Texas Freaks Believed to Have Been
Crossed With White Tail Deer

Special Dispatch to the Globe-Democrat
Cuero, Texas, Dec. 7. – Several specimens of jack rabbits that have evidently been crossed with white tail deer have been killed in this section. These rabbits have well-formed antlers several inches long. Many such jack rabbits have recently also been killed in adjoining counties .

– OUTDOOR LIFE, 1911

57 c

57 b. Colonel George Armstrong Custer and a hunting party of cavalry scouts on the Great Plains in the early 1870s. Custer's personal narrative of a buffalo hunt begins on page 36.

57 c. An elderly Wisconsin deer hunter poses outside his home with a pair of whitetails he bagged on opening day. His Civil War era belt buckle indicates he once served in the Union army.

58

58. "Coyote Smith" and timber wolf, Glenrock, Wyoming.

59 a. Setting a bear trap beside a log cubby, Colorado, date unknown.

59 a

59 b. *"A Long Shot" – an antelope hunter poses upon his horse whose set of tail and ears indicate a disapproving attitude towards horseback gunfire.*

60. *"Skinning the deer," circa 1900. Note the box marked "Kodak" hanging from the tree at center.*

61. *A 1910 deer camp at Chickasha, Oklahoma.*

62. *"Toting" the game – skeeing [sic] in the Bad Lands, Montana," 1902.*

FISHING

2. The caption on this 1908 stereoscopic photo reads, "Steady, Mary, he's a whopper." The photo, taken at Willow River Falls, Wisconsin, indicates women were taking an active role in outdoor sports at the turn of the century. Note the canvas canoe.

FISHING

MY FIGHT WITH A MASCALONGE

It was my good fortune in company with an eastern dry goods salesman named Frank Smith to visit the lakes of northern Wisconsin on a fishing trip.

We had two weeks for the trip, but after spending the greater part of the first week in visiting different lakes, we began to think that we would have to return without the big fish we started after.

The last lake we camped on proved to be an excellent one for wall-eyed pike and mascalonge.

When I awoke in the morning I found that it was but a quarter after 5 and Frank was sound asleep.

I quietly dressed and went down to the boat. There were indications of an approaching storm and quite a sea was running, which made it difficult for me to manage the boat and trolling line. Placing a ballast in the fore part of the boat, I started to cross the lake, but had gone only a few rods when I felt a sudden jerk on my line. Then an unusually large fish leaped about 50 feet from my boat.

I had hooked a mascalonge. I stopped rowing and tried to pull him in, but alas, he would not come.

Thinking that it would be useless to try more, I rowed for deeper water.

After racing him about for 15 or 20 minutes I succeeded in getting my game alongside the boat. Surely, I thought, he must be played out by this time. Taking a firm hold of the line, I tried to lift him into the boat, when there was a quick pull on the line, and I fell overboard.

I soon reappeared and saw that my boat was at least 30 feet from me and was under motion.

Was it drifting? Or was it that the monstrous fish had it in tow? I had fastened my line to the inside of the boat, making it easier to handle the boat. The distance between me and the boat began to widen, and as I was at least three-fourths of a mile from shore, my only hope seemed to be in reaching the boat. I had begun a race for life. The boat would stop and then suddenly go forward. Once I almost reached it, only to see it move away.

I had been swimming some 15 or 20 minutes, and I began to lose hope of ever reaching the boat or shore. I turned over on my back and floated for a rest. When I again assumed a swimming position, I was surprised to find the boat quite near. In a few moments it was within

___

1. Contemporary sporting magazines allude to kite fishing for salt water fish as a relatively recent phenomenon, but this 1911 photograph of Capt. George Farnsworth and his "Kite Tuna Catcher" (invented June 7, 1906, according to the notation on the photograph) proves otherwise.

3

3. A party of fishing guides and their "dudes" on Wisconsin's famous Brule River (about 1900) pause for a photo and to display some of their catch. The guide at far left is holding a fine brace of trout.

4. In 1938, Glacier National Park was a little known wilderness area and the scene for spectacular landlocked salmon and lake trout action.

my reach, and after several unsuccessful attempts, I succeeded in getting inside.

A strong pull on the line, which was still fast to the boat, convinced me that it would be useless to try to bring the fish inside the boat. I looked for my gaff-hook, but it was nowhere to be seen. I then rowed in the direction of camp, and called to Frank. He had neither hat, coat or shoes on.

"Throw out the gaff!" I cried at the top of my voice. He understood and was soon back from the tent with the hook.

By a well-directed throw the hook landed but a short distance from my boat, its wooden handle preventing it from sinking.

I was now sure of landing my fish. Drawing him alongside the boat, I reached over and hooked him.

Zip! the handle went through my fingers and the line in my other hand snapped in two.

The mascalonge now had the gaff-hook, a short piece of line and a number 10 spoon.

My first impression was that I had lost all until I heard Frank's voice.

"The gaff; don't you see the gaff?" I heard him say,

and looking in his direction, I saw the wooden handle dancing on the waves.

"Hurrah!" I cried, as I rowed in the direction of the gaff.

My antagonist was played out completely and all I had to do was to lift him into the boat. The fish tipped the camp scales at an impressive 54-1/2 pounds.

We broke camp next morning and returned home to resume the arduous duties of selling dry goods.

- John A. Miltimore,
FIELD & STREAM, September, 1901

An Auto Fishing Trip

Probably one of the wildest and speediest rides ever taken in an automobile in the Rocky Mountains was made by a party of five who left Palisade, Colo., in a four-cylinder Franklin car at 5 o'clock a.m., July 19, 1911. We reached our destination at the head of the White River, a distance of over 200 miles, at 6:30 p.m. the same day, an hour ahead of the time anticipated. It

5

6

5. *In its earlier days, fly fishing was accomplished with bamboo rods, usually of inferior quality, silk lines and imported wet flies. Because of the less-refined tackle in use at the time, the sport was not as popular as it is today.*

6. *Two Idaho trout fishermen trudge home at the end of a successful day's fishing. The angler wearing the campaign hat (right) sports a .45 "long" Colt revolver on his hip.*

7. *An Oregon trout fisherman, equipped with an early model automatic fly reel, fights a big trout to the finish.*

8. *A pair of anglers working white water for trout. By the size of the wicker creel worn by the fisherman on the right, expectations for a large catch were high.*

9. *"A.A. Cass and the big trout, July 12, 1914" is the notation on the back of this photo taken in an Oregon photographer's studio.*

10. Four lady anglers ice fish for walleyes on a Minnesota lake, circa 1925.

11. Finely turned-out ladies and their gentlemen escorts fishing near Wagon Wheel Gap, Colorado (date unknown).

12. An Idaho angler puts a full bend into the rod as her partner assists by netting her catch, circa 1915.

13. Fishing the riffles on Colorado's Rio Grande, date unknown.

15

14. *Previous spread: "A view of Carey Pond, Adirondacks," 1881.*

15. *"Jonah Jr. and Jewfish, Catalina Island, California," 1909 .*

16. *F.S. Schenk poses with his rod and reel world record black sea bass (384 pounds) taken off Catalina Island, California in 1900.*

Black Sea Bass   The Worlds Record By F.S.Schenck
On   Rod & Reel. WT 384 Lbs Catalina Isl, Cal, Copyright By

16

73

17

18

17 and 18. *"A rush of foam"* and *"High dive by a silver king"* are rare 1926 action photos of tarpon fishing off Venice, Florida.

19

20

20 a

19. *"Leaping tuna hooked 2 p.m., August 9th, 1911 – landed August 10th, 6:57 a.m., off Avalon, California."*

20. *"A thirteen-foot great white shark caught with hook and line, Panama Railroad Dock, City of Panama," circa 1911.*

20 a. *"A veteran angler," 1891, with his tackle bag, tin bait box and no-kidding-around tackle.*

21. *A 632-pound, 10-foot, 11-inch Idaho white sturgeon taken in 1911, probably from the Snake River.*

22. *A pair of big catfish caught in the Washita River two miles east of Chicasha, Oklahoma, circa 1905.*

23. *A fine mess of paddlefish from the Mississippi River, circa 1910.*

was a great ride - one never to be forgotten by those who participated in it. Those in the party were Dana Reed, C.S. Reed, F. Crumly, J.R. Bradshaw and the writer. The trip was made in the writer's machine, and the experiences at times were thrilling, our ride taking us down the mountain sides and on the edges of precipices where many dangers lurked. We followed up the Grand River to Plateau Creek, thence to De Beque and on to Grand Valley over a road that wound up a steep mountain like a snake. Down the other side the auto speeded, at times making sharp curves, where the wheels grazed the edges of an abyss by only a few inches; then into the open, where sagebrush and dust were about all that could be seen in any direction. The dust clung to the sides of the car and to the occupants until all looked a mass of grey.

Nearing Rifle, we found the rocks thick and the curves of the road sharp, but time in our case was valuable, and the town was passed at noon, the auto breaking all records in the run to Meeker.

About twelve miles beyond the latter town an incident occurred which the occupants of the car will not soon forget: The rocks were thicker than usual and the curves sharper. Then suddenly we came upon a big rock, and at forty miles an hour the machine was charged full upon it. The auto lurched to one side, slipped sideways in the sand, but cleared the turn in style, when the writer, glancing over his shoulder, saw the pebbles that had slipped from beneath the wheels falling over the 500-foot bluff just left behind. At 5:30 p.m. the car came to a stop twenty-five miles up the White River from Meeker, in front of a cabin known as Denton's Rest, one of the greatest trout streams in the Rocky Mountains.

The following morning at 7 o'clock Messrs. C.S. Reed, D. Reed, Bradshaw and the writer with line and rod started to test our respective abilities as fishermen. It being my first trip on the White River, I was skeptical and hardly expected to get trout enough to eat, but one Mr. Charles Reed had guaranteed us all the trout the party could eat, so it was up to him to make good. Some went upstream and some down. When I came in at 11 o'clock I had just one small trout. The balance of the boys did not get in until 2 or 3 o'clock in the afternoon, but they were all well rewarded, as Bradshaw had twenty-one, D. Reed twenty-three and Charles Reed twenty-seven - all fine ones.

After dinner we fished near the cabin, all being quite successful.

Next morning we arose early and fished hard all day, getting the usual three good trout meals from Mrs. Denton's table. Then we took our catch - a fine bunch of trout - and strung it up with bailing wire and hung it over night. In the morning we loaded our fish in a box and started for Meeker. As it was July we were making a mad rush for Meeker - and ice. We landed in Meeker at 9:45, where we got fifty pounds of ice and put it under and around our fish, and started for Palisade, which we made after a good deal of trouble. But we brought with us the finest bunch of mountain trout that has ever been

24. *Choctaw Indians shooting fish, most likely carp, with bows and arrows in Oklahoma, 1902.*

24

28

25. *A member of this Iowa fishing party (center) plays cornet for the entertainment of the camp members.*

26. *Black bass for shore lunch, circa 1928.*

27. *Circa 1895 fishing outing in Idaho.*

28. *A Pennsylvania fishing party "By the Campfire," 1897.*

29. *"Flippin' flapjacks," the camp cook's perennial floor show.*

29

taken into Palisade, and the party had one of the finest fishing trips of their lives. We had been gone from home only four days and had covered 400 miles of interesting country in one of the grandest parts of Colorado.

- OUTDOOR LIFE, circa 1912

Trouting Outfit

Editor – What would you advise a beginner to buy as his first trouting outfit?

F.J.M.

A four-dollar lancewood flyrod, a dollar common-click (no multiplier) reel, a dozen silk gut leaders, a dollar creel (shoulder basket), and two dozen assorted flies from the workshop of a maker who is a fly-fisherman as well as a fly tier. Later you may use a fifty-dollar split bamboo rod if you wish, but it won't last any longer, bend any better, take any more trout, or look any prettier than the lancewood article – if you take care of it. Don't buy a cheap, machine-made bamboo rod. These are used only as dining room decorations. If you can't afford a genuine hand-made split bamboo, take a moderate-price lancewood (two dollars to six dollars) or a greenheart (three dollars to ten dollars). Whichever you choose, buy it at a regular tackle store where the men behind the counter use tackle as well as sell it. Don't take any tackle on the advice of the never-go-fishing dry goods clerks. They don't know and don't care to know a trout rod from a table leaf.

OUTDOOR LIFE, circa 1909

---

30. Idaho salmon fishing in the late 1920s. The rifle leaning against the rear fender of the car was, no doubt, for "bear insurance."

31. Fishermen near the Dalles of the St. Louis River on the Wisconsin-Minnesota border, about 1899. The fragile birch-bark canoes and the Duluth packs on the two anglers on the right were standard gear for campers of this period.

32. "Landing a 34-pound Mascalonge" (muskellunge).

33. A "rough but ready campsite," complete with lean-to, will shelter this adventurous trio during their northwoods fishing vacation

30

33

31

32

3288

*33. b, c. A well-provisioned Wyoming fishing-hunting camp on
wheels, circa 1912.*

34

36

35

37

34. *This swarthy fishermen looks out over Cordova Bay, Alaska, where he took this impressive catch of halibut. Date unknown.*

35. *A day's catch of smallmouth bass and two northern pike adorn this Vermont angler's boathouse. After he caught these dandies and before the picture was taken, however, he obviously changed attire to be more photogenic.*

36. *Fishing a run on an Adirondack brook trout stream.*

37. *A lazy afternoon's fishing in Idaho, 1915.*

38

39

40

41

38. Four "boys of summer" near Gordon, Wisconsin, 1903.

39. "In boyhood's happy hours," 1901.

40. Two barefoot Minnesota farm boys wile away an afternoon, bank fishing for walleyes.

41. A quartet of Tom Sawyers, Mercer County, Missouri, 1896.

42. This sentimental rural portrait was not perfect enough for the photographer who, through retouching, added rings around the bobber.

43 and 44. *On big water or small, fishing holds an eternal attraction for youngsters.*

FORESTS & UPLANDS

2. "The Critical Moment," 1895. The low tail-set of the dogs is somewhat typical of many pointing breeds of the era.

FORESTS & UPLANDS

FARMERS AND SPORTSMEN

Peotone, ILL., March 24, 1877

Editor, Chicago Field: – As matters are going now I am afraid that the time is not very far distant when, instead of enjoying real sport, the sportsman will have to lay his gun aside and depend wholly on reminiscences of his imagination.

There is a great deal of quiet amusement to be had in these same things of the past or in "building castles in the air" for the future; but one likes to think over them in the proper season, viz.: winter when all out of door sport is prohibited by Jack Frost, and not in the Spring or Fall when one should be out with his faithful dog, none the less faithful because he *may* or *may not* be a blue blood, a native, or a dropper, dealing death to snipe, quail, grouse, etc.

What leads me to write the above is, that I have been looking over the game laws of most of the different States, and in some of them I find that, after making the penalties severe for shooting out of season, a clause is inserted giving owners of land a right to shoot game on their own premises. I believe this virtually makes the law a dead letter as far as protecting the game is concerned. It prevents the sportsman from shooting at certain times (though I do not believe that any man

calling himself a true sportsman would shoot any game bird during the breeding season, or while the young brood were dependent on their parents for sustenance) but I can not see any difference in the amount of injury done the birds by shooting out of season, because it is a farmer who does, and not a sportsman, though probably the birds would have some slight show of escape with the sportsman but not with the farmer, the former shooting on the wing, and the latter generally preferring to make a good haul by shooting into the bevy as it is huddled together on the ground. In either case a nest of eggs or a young brood would be as effectually destroyed as though they were broken or had their necks wrung respectively.

Many farmers have the idea that the law is made not for the purpose of preventing the total extinction of the game, but with the sole object of allowing shooting only when the sportsman can find time to attend to it. This is, of course, absurd, but you can't make them believe anything else, and they'd rather see the "old one" and all his imps than a sportsman with his dog and gun. The farmers complain that by the time they can get into the field the game is either all shot or has become so wild as to preclude the possibility of a shot. This is doubtless true in part, but if farmers would look at the matter in a reasonable light, leaving the sportsman out, they could

1. An attractive lady hunter, dressed in her 1915-style sporting wardrobe.

3   4

5

3. "Prairie chicken shooting in the South Dakota wheatfields," a 1906 stereograph.

4. Companion print to photo 3, "Brought to hand, a faithful servant."

5. "Before the fox hunt," Virginia. Date unknown.

6. "Quail hunters at lunch time," 1898.

...... 3253. Quail Hunters at Lunch Time.

6

not fail to see that some law was necessary, and that it was for their interest to uphold and observe the law, even if they never shot a bird. Quails and grouse do the farmer immense service in clearing his land of bugs injurious to his crops, and if he were to calculate how many of these pests would one brood of ten or twelve birds devour in a season, he would never taste game rather than shoot in the Spring or Summer. What I have said above applies to one class of farmers; there is another class who will never allow a quail to be killed on their farms. This is the other extreme, and I propose below a plan which will place farmers and sportsmen in pleasanter terms, and be for their mutual benefit.

Let the sportsmen in every town invite the farmers to join their club as honorary members. The farmers agreeing to allow no one but members to shoot over their farms, and the club agreeing to be responsible for all damage done to crops, etc.; also agreeing to prosecute all trespassers and law-breakers. If a member has a friend whom he wishes should enjoy the privilege of a shoot over any of the farms, let him fill out a blank like the following:

Peotone Sportsman's Club.
Mr. _____ . Allow the bearer, Mr. John Smith, to shoot over your farm. I will be responsible for all damages.

Signed by member giving it.

Now if John Smith has the misfortune to do any damage, the farmer calls on him for payment, if he is unable or unwilling to pay, the signer of the pass is

obliged to do so, and John Smith's name is placed on a black list, and he can get no more shooting in that vicinity without incurring the risk of being treated as a trespasser.

The above is not copyrighted nor is it original. Nevertheless, I believe it is an excellent idea, and that it would do more to bring farmers and sportsmen together than anything else. It is, or was, in force in DeKalb County, in this State, and worked well I understand.

The great trouble is that farmers class together all men who shoot which is manifestly as unjust to the true sportsman (who is always a gentleman) as to place professional billiard *sharpers* in the same category. A true sportsman regards the rights of others. He will not go upon a field of grain regardless of damage, for the sake of a shot or two; neither will he spend half an hour in tearing down a length of fence to save himself the trouble of climbing over, leaving it down behind him, as I have heard farmers accuse them of doing. Such men would not be recognized as *sportsmen* and are either pot hunters or snobs out for a holiday.

A sportsman will not shoot a cow because he mistakes it for a deer, he knows a little too much of natural history for that, nor to see if he can hit it; he is always averse to inflicting needless pain on any animal; he shoots for amusement and the health which field sports always give their devotees, and will leave the field in the midst of good shooting rather than kill more game than he and his friends can use.

When some such arrangement as suggested above is made, complete harmony will be restored between farmers and sportsmen, and you will not hear a farmer

95

7. *"A group of pheasant hunters. Salem, S.D., Year 1926,"* in the *heyday of prairie pheasant populations when fields erupted with hundreds of flushing roosters.*

8. *A mixed bag from the South Dakota prairie, circa 1926.*

9. *These pilots flew their biplanes from Michigan and Chicago to sample the heralded prairie pheasant shooting, circa 1926.*

10. *An interesting Otto M. Johnson photo of 1925 showing a pheasant gunner on the Idaho prairie.*

7

8

9

exclaim on seeing a man with a dog and gun get off the train in his town, "Wal, I must get home, get up the cows, shut up the hens, and put the pigs and sheep into shelter, for there's one of them darned city chaps come down here shootin'."

Hoping that the sportsmen's clubs over the country will consider this proposition.

I remain your friend.
T. Umbellus

TURKEY SHOOTING
By Lazy Alic

As this is the height of gobbling time with the turkeys, I concluded the first of last week to give them a turn. I invited my friend Brown who is a true sportsman and "to the manor born" to accompany me.

Tuesday evening, after dinner, all things being in readiness, we left town for the thickets, about ten miles distance. Brown was on horse back, with double barrel gun and ammunition, turkey caller in pocket. I was in my buggy with the buffalo robes, blankets and commissary stores. In addition I set my double barrel gun for turkeys in the morning and evening, and my rifle, thinking I might get a chance at a deer at long range. Away we went in the finest of spirits, bent on sport; we had gone six or seven miles from town to where the wagon road turns away to the left, to get around some branches and thickets to again come into the due course, say two miles distant. There was a blind path or bridle way that went directly across the road. I said to Brown, you take that by-path, now go very slow, and keep your eye skinned, for the first thing you know

11

12

13

13 a

11. *Wide open in Idaho, 1915.*

12. *West-central Minnesota, 1913.*

13. *Grouse hunting in central Wisconsin, circa 1916. Note the hump-backed Belgian Browning shotguns.*

13 a. *Fording a slough, Idaho.*

you will ride right upon a drove of deer or a gang of turkeys; but should you see the game, you will beat me to where the trail intersects the wagon road, in which event you can hitch your horse to a tree and slip up the branch to some small prairies where you may see some game, as it is a charming place for deer and turkeys to stay.

Sure enough, when I got round there was Brown's horse, hitched as I had told him. I drew in my reins, and had not waited more than eight or ten minutes until I heard the report of Brown's gun. In a few minutes he came walking back with a fine, young two-year-old gobbler on his back, beard about four inches long. I tell you he was a beauty; the gobbler was drawn, gizzard, liver and heart stowed away inside of him for camp meat; the skin was split on his breast, and the crop taken out; for at this time of the year the wild onions are up five or six inches high, and when the crop is left in the dead turkey it generally tastes of the onions. Some salt was thrown inside to season the tidbits and draw the blood from the turkey. The dead turkey was thrown into the buggy. Brown mounted his horse, and half an hour's drive brought us to our camp ground; horses were

14

picketed, wood collected for fire at night, commissary stores and blankets hung up in the trees, and we were ready for the evening's hunt.

from THE CHICAGO FIELD, May 25, 1877

SLAUGHTERING DOVES

-On Tuesday last R.H. Lindsay and A. Maitland met with extraordinary success while dove-shooting at Hot Springs Station, nineteen miles east of Wadsworth, on the line of the Central Pacific Railroad. The two sportsmen killed 380 birds in one day. The doves come to the place to drink, and when about a quarter of a million are gathered round to drink, the two Nimrods, who are secreted in a bath-house about thirty yards away, cautiously poke their guns through a hole in the wall and blaze away with four barrels; then they get out and rake up the game in baskets. The brakemen on the Central Pacific Railroad occasionally hunt the doves here with hand missiles or clubs. One brakeman killed ten doves with a single throw of a coupling pin.

from the VIRGINIA CHRONICLE, circa 1877

"ON QUAIL WITHHOLDING SCENT"

Of all the birds in this or any other country, so far as I know from personal experience, or have heard from others more competent to pronounce on the subject, the Quail is the most difficult both to find and to kill with certainty.

When flushed in the open, these birds immediately fly to the thickest and most impenetrable covert they can find; and in some sections of the country in which I have shot, Maryland especially, that covert is of such a nature, so interwoven with parasitic creepers, cat briars, and wild vines, and so thickly set with knotted and thorny brushwood, that they can run with impunity before the noses of your Pointers and Setters, and that, without the aid of cocking spaniels, which are little used in the United States, they cannot be forced to take wing.

These birds have another singular quality, which renders them exceedingly difficult to find, even when they have been accurately marked down after being once flushed. It is, that for some considerable time after they have alighted, they give forth no scent whatsoever,

and that the very best dogs will fail to give any sign of their presence.

Whether this retention of scent is voluntary on the part of the bird, it is very difficult to ascertain. It is a very strange power, if it be voluntary, yet no more strange than many others of the instincts possessed by wild animals.

Frank Forester, from FRANK FORESTER'S FIELD SPORTS, VOL. 1, 1852

DO QUAIL WITHHOLD THEIR SCENT?

Des Moines, Iowa, Jan. 25, 1877. – *Editor, Chicago Field:* – In the Chicago Field of the 27th, inst., Mr. Arnold Burges, in a very good article says: "We all know too that quails do at times withhold their scent so as to baffle the keenest nosed dog." I fail to be one of the "all" who recognize this supposed fact.

It is true I have seen good dogs baffled, when I could not readily account for it, but this thing of scent is not deemed to be a faculty capable of being exercised at will by the quail or any other bird or animal. I shall not now attempt to discuss this question, but as the statement comes in direct form, and from a source so capable of giving a reason for the faith that is in him, I would be pleased to have a satisfactory explanation of the "fact," if one can be given on philosophical and physiological grounds.

We should not attempt to account for the pretty weather we now have, as a gentleman did last evening, by saying, "The moon runs so high," and I do not believe that Mr. Burges deals in that kind of moonshine.

Yours truly,

Eland

HOW AND WHY QUAIL WITHOLD THEIR SCENT

Hillsdale, April 6, 1877
Editor, Chicago Field: – Sickness must be my apology to "Eland" for this delay in giving him my views upon the question of quails withholding their scent, to which I

14.*Preceding spread: Local hunting gentry with their fine doubles, dogs and the chef of Pierce House (Vermont) gather with their bag of grouse, woodcock and rabbits. Date unknown.*

COPYRIGHTED BY
T. W. INGERSOLL, 1900.

.....3268. All Ready for the Rise, Chicken Shooting

15

16

15. "All Ready for the Rise, Chicken Shooting," 1900. Again, setters' tails set low.

16. Dr. G.T. Page of Sioux Falls, S.D., moves in to flush. Circa 1900.

17. "Quail shooting in the stubble – A Point – Look Out," 1891. 'Look out,' indeed, for the hunter at left has his double levelled squarely on the temple of his partner!

18. A proud owner poses with his stylish team of setters, circa 1920.

briefly referred in a late issue of the CHICAGO FIELD. "Eland" asks if I "believe in such moonshine," and I emphatically say I do believe, nay more I *know* that quails have this faculty, but I do not claim that it is one the birds can exercise at will. In other words, I do not consider this a voluntary exhibition, but one induced and controlled by external circumstances.

I have gained my knowledge of the fact that quails *do* withhold their scent, by a quarter of a century's practical experience, during which I have times without number seen both bevies and single birds marked down with the utmost exactitude, yet passed over without the slightest notice by the best nosed and most careful dogs I have ever seen in the field. I can recall several cases where I have marked a bird settle by the side of a stone or tuft of grass and after the dogs had failed to find him, though made to hunt every foot of ground about the place, have discovered the skulker crouched just where I had seen him alight, and have flushed him within a yard of dogs of unquestionably superior scenting powers. I could quote many recognized authorities who assert that quails do withhold their scent, but of them all, no one will have greater weight than that true sportsman, close observer and shrewd critic Frank Forester. To save time and space I will refer "Eland" and other doubters to Forester's *Field Sports*, pages 226 and 269; also to "My Shooting Box," by the same author, pages 63 to 67. The most absurd and senseless argument I have ever heard or read of, advanced to prove that quail do not withhold their scent, I find in that egotistical record of personal prowess, "Field Cover and Trap Shooting" by Capt. Bogardus – wherein he says as a reason that dogs do not

Quail shooting in the stubble—A point—Look out.

Copyright 1891 by Geo. Barker.

17

18

19

A 'Possum Hunt. The 'Possum Viewing His Finish.

20

19. *Southern hunters, circa 1895, pose with their guns (two of them Civil War vintage muzzle-loaders), hound and their quarry – a raccoon.*

20. *"A Possum Hunt. The 'Possum Views His Finish," circa 1895.*

21. *"Treed," date unknown.*

find all the birds of a bevy, "It is not a question of no scent, but of too much. The bevy have been lying there and running all over the ground, so that it is covered and tainted with scent to such a degree that the noses of the dogs become full of it, and that is why they cannot find and put up one or two birds which lie close." I have never known before that any one has claimed quails withheld their scent when feeding and moving about. It is only *after being flushed* that this faculty is called into action, but the author in his anxiety to impress upon the public his own abilities as a bird butcher, loses sight of all less important matters and makes himself ridiculous in this manner. Perhaps I am wrong to waste time in exposing such a blunder, but as I have twice heard Bogardus' book gravely quoted as authority, I have deemed it best to show how little claim it has upon the consideration of educated sportsmen....

Arnold Burges

CAN QUAILS WITHHOLD THEIR SCENT?

Editor, Chicago Field: – The theory that the quail can retain its scent is an exception to a general rule, seemingly contrary to reason, and it should not, therefore, be credited except on indisputable evidence.

It is true, however, that there is something mysterious about scent; for instance, it is an admitted fact, I believe, that the young of the deer kind cannot be trailed by wolves or the best of dogs, yet the only explanation we can give for the fact is that it is inherent.

It is a fact well known to huntsmen that no animal, however acute its scent may be, can scent a man, say

22

22 & 23. *Idaho, 1914. Otto M. Johnson photo of a frog hunting party and their gallery model .22's.*

24. *Wild turkeys from the swamps of southern Florida, about 1920.*

23

fifteen feet above it. The cause is apparent and easily explained, but I mention it as a fact which, in my opinion, has a bearing on the main question; the quail on the wing does not leave sufficient scent within the scope of a dog's scenting power to enable him to follow it, and when it darts down into dense cover and there remains with close-lying feathers the best of dogs will sometimes fail to find it.

My own observation constrains me to believe that this is about the limit of the quail's power to retain its scent. I have too much confidence in *my* dogs to doubt their ability to find a quail if it leaves behind it a trail.

I am pleased to believe that "Eland," of Des Moines is skeptical in regard to the quail's power to withhold its scent. I think, if he ever had any doubt on the subject, his dogs have taught him better. I remember his famous old pointer, Bill, who, in days by-gone, used to rush into my office like a rifle ball and nose my gun and look at me in a chiding way which seemed to say; "Let the all-

mighty dollar go to thunder for the nonce and let's be off to the stubble and hake."

John J. Brompton

CAN QUAILS WITHOLD SCENT?

Hills of Linganore, Md., April 2, 1877

Editor, Chicago Field: – I noticed a communication in the CHICAGO FIELD in the issue of the 31st of March headed "Can Quail Withhold Their Scent?" and signed by John J. Brompton. In this communication Mr. Brompton quotes from "Lewis' American Sportsman," "Frank Forester's Manual for Young Sportsmen," "Adam Bogardus' Field Cover and Trap Shooting," and "Frank Schley's American Partridge and Pheasant Shooting." Mr. Brompton gives each of these authors' views about quails withholding their scent, as he quotes them from

25. *"American Eagle, 7 ft. from tip to tip. Killed by J.A. Ryal, Feb. 10, 1915," Oklahoma. Attitudes towards avian predators have changed greatly over the years. In the early part of this century, eagles and other raptors were considered vermin and shot on sight.*

26. *Playful lady hunters tote their game home, Idaho, 1915.*

27. *A 1902 "trick" stereograph: "A Wing Shot – Quail Hunting in the West, U.S.A."*

28. *Cross Plains, Wisconsin, raccoon hunters, circa 1930.*

30

31

29. *This touching studio portrait evokes images of boyhood friendships and woodlot hunts of a bygone era. Otto Radke, Andrew Eckstein and Jake Lange pose with their single-shot 12 gauges and a mixed bag of squirrels, rabbits and grouse. 1920s.*

30. *"After the Hunt," date unknown; boys, beagles an bunnies.*

31. *"Shooting the Pheasant," 1900. A curious stereo of a boy levelling his gun on a perched grouse as the terrier at his feet gazes at the barrel.*

32

33

32. This is either a remarkably short Adirondacks hunter of 1891 or an especially large ruffed grouse!

33. Hunting party or posse? Hounds, horses and men – mounted and ready. Date unknown.

34. "30 Minute Hunt," Idaho, circa 1910. These jackrabbits appear bigger than the dog, who didn't sit still long enough for proper photo exposure.

34

35 a

35 b

35 c

35. a, b, c. Idaho trick shot Mrs. Topperwein shoots empty shotgun shells off her husbands fingers and clay targets out of the air with a revolver, 1915.

their own pen, and names the number of the page in each volume where the subject can be found. Mr. Brompton awards the palm after reading all the above works on the subject and is of the opinion that Frank Schley's "American Partridge and Pheasant Shooting" on page 83 gives conclusive reasons for the belief that quails cannot withhold their scent.

Now, Mr. Editor, right here I want to say a word which is simply this, I have read articles in the *Rod and Gun* time and again. I have read articles in the *Forest and Stream* and also in the CHICAGO FIELD about quails withholding their scent until I am heartily tired of the subject, but I must say to do the author and work justice, that "Frank Schley's American Partridge and Pheasant Shooting" on page 83 and 84 in my opinion gives the best, most practicable and most conclusive and substantial reasons that quails cannot withhold their scent, that I have ever seen, or ever expect to see in print. And I fully agree with Mr. Schley in his views, and with Mr. Brompton on this subject, that Mr. Schley has explained this problem in his estimable work on partridge and pheasant shooting, in a masterly and skillfully, and in my opinion, in a very satisfactory and conclusive manner, that the quail cannot withhold its scent.

Justice

In regard to this matter, we are forced to exclaim, "Hold, enough!" – Editor

THIRTY-THREE QUAILS

– Mr. Thomas Hackett, of Sedalia, Mo., for a wager of $50 has eaten thirty quails in thirty consecutive days. Owing to a misunderstanding when the task should commence, Mr. Hackett ate thirty-three, being three more quails than wagered for.

from THE CHICAGO FIELD, 1877

117

35 d

d. Trap shooting in Idaho, 1915, and (e) in Iowa, circa 1910.

He Goes For Lazy Alic

Oskaloosa, Iowa, May, 1877

Editor, Chicago Field: – In your issue of May 19th, 1877, I noticed a communication from "Lazy Alic," of McKinney, Texas, describing a wild turkey hunt in his part of the country in the Spring of the year. He goes on and describes the sport in glowing terms. I do not know what the game laws of Texas are, or whether they have any at all, but I do think that any man that makes any pretensions towards being a sportsman ought to know better than to kill wild turkeys in the Spring of the year. In our part of the country it costs any person the nice little sum of $10 to do a job of that kind, besides getting the ill will of the whole sporting community. "Lazy Alic" goes on and tells about the gobblers eating wild onions and says the crop has to be taken out as soon as the turkey is killed to prevent the meat from tasting like the onions. I do not doubt the eating of the onions but as to the taste of the meat I think differently. I will ask "Lazy Alic" if he ever ate a piece of an old buck during the rutting season; and if so, did not the meat have a very strong, disagreeable taste, and was not the neck of the deer swollen to twice the natural size? It is just so with the old gobblers in the Spring if the year. During the treading season the neck becomes enlarged and the whole breast is very much swollen, rendering the turkey,

in my estimation, wholly unfit to eat. And as to the skill, "Lazy Alic" says it requires to kill an old gobbler at this season of the year, I think he shoots wide of the mark, for there is not a school boy in the country anywhere who does not know that if he can imitate the call of the hen turkey at all, he can betray the gobblers during the treading season. If I was in "Lazy Alic's" place and made a practice of killing turkeys in the Sprig of the year, I would keep it to myself and not let sportsmen know anything about it, for no sportsman will hear of it but to condemn. With the best of feelings toward brother "Alic," I will close, hoping the next time he kills an old gobbler that it will be in the Fall of the year instead of the Spring.

Rifle Shot
from THE CHICAGO FIELD, 1877

Ten Gauge vs. Rifle Shot

Corinth, Miss., July 1, 1877

Editor, Chicago Field: – It is really amusing at times to read the learned discussion of some of the "mighty hunters" on the subject of hunting the different kinds of game scattered through our country. Especially the

lecture they see fit to read to some poor devil "away down South in Dixie," in the huge impropriety of hunting at times which are said, by them, to be out of season, the turkey, deer or quails. But when one of them spreads himself as did "Rifle Shot" in a recent number of the CHICAGO FIELD, on hunting gobblers in the Spring, a subject about which he knows evidently as much as a pig knows of the language of the Hebrews, it is time to "call him" and ascertain if it is only a joke, or if he means business.

"Rifle Shot's" article contained more errors and displayed more *total depravity* than anything published since Twain's last. Where did he learn that any schoolboy in the country knows "that if he can imitate the call of the hen turkey at all, he can *betray* the gobblers during the treading season"? He surely has been trying his hand on some old bronze gobbler in the back yard of some farm house, and has never seen a wild turkey in the woods, much less "betrayed" one during the treading.

As to what constitutes sport, tastes differ, and each one is entitled to his own opinion. Some call it sport to wait at a deer stand until the game is driven almost over them and then shoot it down with a scatter gun, others call it sport to shoot squirrels near enough for their eye lashes to be seen. Others again see no sport in anything which is not shot on the wing over dogs.

"Rifle Shot" also compares the flesh of a gobbler during the Spring to that of an old buck during rutting time. My dear fellow sportsmen, try a fat chicken of the "male persuasion," or the indolent husband of some duck, and learn that there is a cast difference between an animal and bird during "treading season."

I am well aware that many sportsmen, good and true, consider it not quite the thing to shoot turkeys during gobbling time; but I am sure they are mistaken. And in all sincerity, if you wish to test to the utmost, all your boasted reason, skill, and ingenuity as a hunter, why tackle an old gobbler who has "heard a cap pop" and his educated instinct will show the wiliest hunter of them all, inducements sufficient to persuade him to go home gobblerless. Try as you may, use all your skill in the use of the call, and the many arts and tricks you have been taught; one false note, the least unusual noise, the waving of a leaf, or even the excited note of a bird, is enough to put gallipavo on the *qui vive,* and even Rifle Shot might then fail to betray him.

As to the difference in Spring hunting which he so much condemns, and Fall hunting which he allows, it is easier by all odds to kill turkeys in the Fall.

Ten Gauge

WATERFOWL

2. *"The Last Man In" is the title of this old stereograph. This Minnesota waterfowler's left oar appears broken, but is actually a rare, jointed, reversible oar that allows the rower to proceed in the direction he is facing while using a conventional rowing stroke.*

WATERFOWL

JANESVILLE NOTES

Janesville, Wis., April 9, 1877

Editor, Chicago Field: – During the past week duck shooting has been better at Lake Koshkonong than for several previous years. At the Black Club House several members have bagged from 50 to 100 per day, about half being canvasbacks. At Bingham the various boarders have done equally as well. Last Wednesday Frank Gray of Janesville and Eddie Bingham bagged over 150; forty-five being canvasbacks, and the same day E.E. Ayer, of Harvard, bagged seventy odd. The ice in the lake is twenty inches thick, and the birds are obliged to seek the shore to get into water. Sportsmen wishing to try canvasback shooting should take the Chicago and Northwestern Railroad, Wisconsin Division, to Koshkonong Station, and wagon conveyance from there to Ira Bingham's, where unexcelled accommodations can be secured. I see C.L. Valentine advertises his decoys in your paper, and having used them, I can recommend them as the best I have used, being painted far superior to other makes.

N.B. – C.L.V. is not a relative of min, neither am I interested in his business.

Yours truly,

Richard Valentine

NIGHT GUNS ON THE CHESAPEAKE

For many years prior to 1883, night shooting with big guns was practiced in the neighborhood of Havre de Grace by a gang of poachers, against whom the processes of the law were invoked in vain. These men went out at night in skiffs, in the bow of which were mounted these great guns, and slaughtered the ducks by thousands on their roosting beds.

These guns, which were commonly known as "night guns," are huge single-barrel shotguns, patterned after an ordinary shotgun, but weighing sometimes 150 pounds, with a bore considerably over an inch in diameter. Such a gun was mounted on a pivot in the bow of a small skiff, to be paddled through the water, or which might be mounted on runners and pushed over the ice. The stock of the gun was braced against a block in the boat, and the recoil of the discharge often sent the boat back a long way through the water. The gun was usually painted the same color as the boat, some dull, inconspicuous tint. For many years there have been laws prohibiting the killing of ducks by this means, and many efforts had been made to convict the persons who were known to practice this illegal gunning. For this reason, each gun was so mounted in its boat that it could be easily detached from its fittings, and each had a long string attached to it, running to a buoy, so that in case of

---

1. *Opening day, 1940. A southern Illinois duck hunter waits for his next opportunity to shoot.*

an alarm the arm could be pitched overboard, and the owner paddle away, to return for his property at a later day.

The number of birds killed by the discharge of one of these guns was, of course, very great. The common load was from a quarter to a third of a pound of powder and one and a half to two pounds of shot. The gunner paddled up quietly to the raft of sleeping canvas-backs, adjusted his gun to suit himself and discharged it, sometimes gathering from 75 to 100 ducks as the result.

– From George Bird Grennell's
AMERICAN DUCK SHOOTING, 1901

PRICES OF WILD GAME IN 1873, NEW YORK CITY

The following are the wholesale prices of game in Fulton Market on Tuesday, the 9th December: – Swans, each, $2; wild geese, each, 75 cents; brant, $1.50; canvas backs, $1 a pair; red heads and black ducks, 75c. a pair; mallards, 75 cents a pair; broad bills, pair, 50 cents; teal, pair, 50 cents; widgeon, 50 cents; pinnated grouse, pair, 90 cents; woodcock, pair, $1; English snipe, pair, 50 cents; quail, trapped, $1.50 a dozen; wild turkey, 15 cents a pound; wild pigeons per dozen, $1.50; wild rabbits, pair, 40 cents. Game is quite low in consequence of the unusual mild weather. Deer legs, 11 cents; saddles, 18 cents; haunch, 20 cents; bear, coming in.

– FOREST AND STREAM magazine,
December 11, 1873

HIAWATHA NOTES

Hiawatha, Kansas, March 17, 1877. – *Editor, Chicago Field:* – The ducks and geese are giving us quite a benefit and we are having some first-class sport although the bags have not been large. Two of us gave them a matinee from 4 to 6 o'clock one day last week and killed 19 mallards and one snipe (Wilson's), being the first of the season. The show for chickens is good as far as I can judge at this season of the year, and the country will be simply flooded with quails if nothing happens to the young birds. W., from Boone, Iowa, was much surprised to see teal ducks so early; they have been here for some time. The red-heads, whistlers, blue-bills, widgeons, etc., came first; then the teals with a few mallards, and the bulk of the latter a little later.

Chill Shot

DUCK SHOOTING IN FLORIDA

Louisville *Courier Journal*, circa 1878
Ocala, Florida: – How they kill ducks on Lake Wier is known all over Florida, but from some cause I did not hear of it until I had been in the State several weeks. But so soon as I heard of it I struck for the noted place to see the show. Between Lake Wier and Little Lake there is a neck of land thirty feet wide by half a mile long. the duck hunters, sometimes as many as twenty, are strung up and down this neck of land. There they stand in wire grass up to their necks, armed with long poles, having strong lines about six feet long with four-ounce lead balls of lead attached to the little end of the poles, ready for the sport. Other men, who are called grabbers – I suppose because they grab up the dead and wounded – line the beach with their little boats.

About a half hour by sun the ducks begin to come from a large section of country to roost on Lake Wier.

Heavens alive! The ducks, the ducks! I hope I may never see the back of my neck again if I had ever seen such a sight before. You have seen a swarm of bees on the wing; it beats that all "to hollow." After the ducks

3. *"Decoying Wild Ducks – Lying Low,"* circa 1900.

4. *"The Duck Hunters."* 1881, New York State.

5. *"A Morning Over Goose Decoys,"* 1897 stereo.

6. *"Well, What Luck Did You Have?"*

3

4

5

6

7

get to passing the "neck" good, they look like a dark cloud moving for several miles out on the lake. There are more ducks right on and about Lake Wier than in the whole States of Georgia and Alabama combined.

And the noise! Please don't say anything to me about fuss. I have heard whole army trains of wagons passing over a turnpike, "roar of cannons and rattle of musketry." I have heard storms on the waters. But "I will just be Joe Bradley and cry for mush" if I ever heard anything to equal the noise the ducks made flying over. The evening I was there they killed and wounded 1,500, and did not get them all, either. A large number of these fowls are consumed by people living on and around Lake Wier. The wounded – those not badly hurt – have their wings cropped and are turned in a small lake, with a high plank fence around it, made for the purpose. The rest of the ducks are dressed and shipped, it being a fine source of revenue to the place. The duck season begins about November 1st, and lasts until about the middle of March. It is worth a thousand dollars to see the sight.

7. A trio of Minnesota duck hunters warm themselves during a lull in the shooting, 1915.

8. A rather unique stereo, circa 1900, "A Winter Day With the Ducks," which includes two ducks in flight over the decoys.

9. Silver Creek, Idaho, duck hunt, December 1912.

CLEANING A GUN

– Mr. William Vie, of St. Louis, writes: "The best method I know of for cleaning the barrels of a gun is to wipe them out with turpentine. I would like to know whether other sportsmen have tried it. In loading shells I have found that 5 drs. No. 2 DuPont's duck powder, one Ely felt wad and a large wad of wood shavings, such as is packed around furniture and marble, or take brush scrapings on powder, and 1-1/3 No. 6 shot in No. 10 bore, 10 lbs is the best for duck shooting."

from THE CHICAGO FIELD, 1877

8

9

10

American and Foreign Views.

Sold only by Canvassers.

T. W. Ingersoll, Publisher.

56 E. 6th St., St. Paul, Minn., U. S. A.

...... 3239. The Crowd's Return After the Morning Shoot.

11

DUCK SHOOTING IN THE OLD DAYS

By Fred Kimble

Memory now takes me back more than fifty years to the Illinois River and the happiest days of my life, and I seem to see the old camp grounds, bluffs, points of timber, bends in the river, sloughs, shooting grounds and everything, just as I saw them in the long, long ago. In 1868 I lived at Chillicothe, 18 miles north of Peoria, on the Illinois River. The river bottoms were low and marshy on the opposite side, and the best of duck shooting was to be found there.

Duck Island marsh and lake, 32 miles below Peoria, was my favorite shooting ground, back as far as 1869. In that year Joe Long, Henry Doty, Alden Wilky and myself started down the river from Chillicothe on a trip to the Sunny South, intending to hunt on our way down the river, hunt during the Winter, and shoot on the Spring flight north in the Spring. We floated down the river in a small houseboat belonging to Wilky. Our first stop was Duck Island and camps of duck hunters were in evidence all along the west bank. We arrived in the night and carried our boats over the ridge that lies between the river and the rice pond. The wild rice was as thick as you ever saw wheat in a field. Other boats had been taken as far as the edge of the pond, but no boat thus far had penetrated more than a boat length into the thick rice. The water was but a few inches in depth, but the soft mud went down to Jericho, I guess, and then some.

Before leaving Chillicothe we had shot in the Crow Creek rice pond and had come prepared for just such an emergency, and each had a push pole, the kind shown in Long's book. The cuts of boats, decoys, batteries and sink box shown in his book were taken from my outfit. With the push poles, or mud sticks, we were enabled to navigate all over the rice pond, while about all our neighbors could do was to climb the willow trees that grew around the edge of the pond and watch the ducks fall as we would kill them above the rice.

We would shoot till noon, then put in the balance of the day picking up, and it was a man-sized job. On coming ashore we would hide our new-fangled push poles under the rice a few feet out from the shore and wade and wallow through the mud, pulling or pushing our boats the rest of the way, to be met by the other hunters. We shot and worked in this way for about two weeks, when the pond froze over and the ducks left for the South, and we followed them as far as New Madrid, Missouri, making the trip down the Illinois and Mississippi Rivers. When we left our duck-shooting friends were still wondering how we could stand it to wade and wallow in the mud, all over the rice pond, day after day as we had done!

Discovery of Choke Boring Guns

We had our camp outfit hauled over to Little River, seven miles from the Mississippi, a famous resort of ducks and geese, where we camped for the Winter. We were in a part of the Sunken Lands district of Missouri,

---

10. A rugged-looking trio of Minnesota duck hunters, circa 1910. The hunter in the center is holding a rather impressive fowling piece, possibly a 6- or 8-gauge double-barrel muzzle-loader.

11. "The Crowd's Return After the Morning Shoot," 1899.

12. "All They Can Stagger Under (Ducks)," 1899.

3246. All They Can Stagger Under. (Ducks.)

12

13

13. *A big shoot. Railroad companies actively advertised hunting opportunities in the West. The "game" on the side of this Pullman car includes several species of ducks and geese, coots, a prairie chicken, shorebirds, hawks, an eagle, a gull, and one red fox.*

14

15

Arkansas, Tennessee and Kentucky, caused by an earthquake in 1811. I had a double-barrel muzzle-loader, built by O.P. Secor of Peoria, and a single-barrel muzzle-loader, built by Joseph Tanks of Boston. Joe had a breech-loader built by Tonks, and Doty had two muzzle-loaders. My two guns were the first guns ever choke-bored; Joe's was the second. Doty's two guns were open shooting guns. The barrels of my Secor gun were too thin to stand much of a choke, but the single gun had a good thick barrel, and Mr. Tonks made a great shooting gun out of it. I bought it because it outshot my double gun.

The single gun would shoot in a 26-inch circle at 40 yards, Joe's breech-loader in a 30-inch circle, and Doty's two guns would scatter four and a half feet. The single gun was good for single ducks up to 70 yards, Joe's breech-loader up to 60 yards, my double gun up to 50 yards, Doty's guns about 40 yards. My reason for describing our guns in detail is because the knowledge of choke-boring spread from these guns to all parts of the civilized world.

Wildfowl Shooting in the Sunken Lands

After we had got settled in our Little River camp we killed a lot of game, both ducks and geese, and shipped to Cincinnati by boat. On certain days the ducks would come out in the big timber, where most of our shots would be over the tops of the cypress trees, fully 200 feet high. I stepped a fallen tree and found it to be 200 feet long. The single gun was the only gun in camp and, in fact, the only gun known that would reach ducks flying over the tops of these cypress trees. I think Alden Wilky was the best shot of any of us, and learned to

16

133

17

18

shoot the single barrel before I did before we had left the Illinois River country. Ducks would cross the Duck Island rice pond over to Clear Lake on the opposite side of the river, but would fly so high as to be out of reach of ordinary guns. Wilky stood on the river ridge on the Clear Lake side one day and started practicing with the old single barrel. After making a few high shots, something like 70 yards, he succeeded in killing one and found it had been struck with quite a number of No. 4 shot, and in a little while, after getting the proper lead, he began to kill them quite regularly. Finally he got so he had no use for any other gun in camp on the Illinois.

While at New Madrid it froze up and the ducks left us the second time, but the geese remained and we gave them the best we had. One day I killed 40 of the big fellows and a number of days I killed upwards of 30 each day. Some of them weighed 12 to 16 pounds and it was about all I could do to get them to camp in my paddle boat. The more I used the old single gun the better I liked it. When we came north in the Spring we stopped off at the mouth of the Sangamon River, just above Browning. Here I had a good chance to practice shooting over the tops of the timber with this gun and was able to shoot it fairly well, killing some days as many as 30 and 40 mallards without a miss. These ducks were all the way from 40 to 70 yards, and it took careful holding and fine calculation to do it. I had sold my double gun and depended on this single-barrel muzzle-loader for all my shooting, until I got the 6-bore muzzle-loader, which became quite famous.

What My Noted Single-Barrel Gun Would Do

I am the man who discovered choke boring as now used by all gun manufacturers. I started experimenting in the gun shop of Charley Stock, in Peoria, Illinois. At first I used musket barrels left over from the Civil War as they were heavy and would stand lots of boring. Then I procured regulation gun barrels to bore after I had obtained results by repeated boring and calipering.

After I had finished boring the 6-bore I found I had a gun good up to 80 yards. I used 6 drams of coarse grain powder and No. 3 shot, 1-1/2 ounces. This gun would

17. "Two Days Shoot on the Platte," Elm Creek, Saline County, Nebraska, about 1912.

18. Mallards and pheasants near Humboldt, South Dakota, circa 1912.

19. The gunners were apparently as proud of this roadster as they were of their bag of mallards. South Dakota, 1935.

20. In the late 1800s, big bags were common for individual hunters.

shoot through an inch board at 40 yards, 1/2-inch board at 60 yards, 1/4-inch board at 80 yards. The velocity up to 40 yards was very great; at 60 yards it slowed down one-half and at 80 yards it had slowed down another half. Therefore it took twice as long for the shot to travel from 40 to 60 yards as from the gun to 40 yards.

Some Duck-Shooting Records

It may interest you to hear of some of the scores made by this old gun, and I will give a few. I killed one day, out in the middle of the Duck Island rice pond (the pond was bare of rice that year), 203 mallards, not more that one to a shot. At another time, shooting form an ice blind, I killed nearly 200. The ducks could see the blind a long ways and would shy off to 60 yards and over, and the shooting was mostly at long shots. I killed 1,920 ducks in a camping trip of 19 days. With my first breech-loader, after my 6-gauge had been barred out at trap-shooting tournaments and I had ceased to use it, I killed one morning before 9 o'clock, 122 wood ducks. This was over on the Spring Lake side. In a blue-wing teal flight in the rice pond I killed 120 in 120 minutes and ran out of shells. I could have got as many more if I had shells. The following week I shot a friendly match with General Hough, in about the same place. We shot until 9 in the morning. I scored 115 blue-wings; Hough killed 37. In the two weeks we shot in the rice pond on our way south I killed between 100 and 200 mallards every day. In a part of a day opposite La Grange I bagged 162 mallards and one afternoon on the Sangamon I scored 160 mallards. The first time I shot my breech-loader I killed 140 mallards, and the first 32 I shot in pairs over the tops of the timber and killed all of them. I have made straight runs of shooting mallards over the timber of 20, 30, 40, 50, without a miss, using the closest shooting gun in the world, the old 6-gauge. This looks like slaughter these days of small limits, but those days there were ducks for all who would work.

On a wager made by my friends I shot a duck-shooting contest with Ross Knapp of Browning, Illinois. He had the choice of shooting grounds and selected tall timber on the Sangamon River. He used a 4-bore single barrel, weighing 17 pounds. I used a small single barrel, 10 gauge. We stood 100 yards apart in shallow water in the timber. We quit at 3 o'clock in the afternoon and the score was Knapp 37; Kimble 137.

George Hughes, of Fonda, Iowa, challenged me to come out and shoot ducks a day with him on the Iowa prairies. He said Illinois River shooting was easy and he wanted me to try something hard. I went out there and we shot one bitter cold, snowy day in March at the ducks going North. We stood all day in ice-cold water. The score: Hughes 37; Kimble 126.

Remarkable Trap-Shooting Scores

After the Spring duck shooting was over in 1872 I took in the Illinois State Shoot, held in Chicago at wild pigeons. It was almost my first experience at the traps. There were 151 entries in the main event and the best pigeon shots in the country were on the grounds, Captain Bogardus among them. I had the old single-barrel, and it was the only muzzle-loader on the grounds. The event was at ten birds, 21 yards rise, gun below the elbow until the bird was on the wing, ties to be shot off at three birds at 26 yards, and if that didn't settle it, miss and out at 31 yards. Only ten men out of the 151 were able to kill ten straight of the swift flying pigeons. After three birds at 26 yards only Bogardus and I were left of the entire field. After we had gone straight for 20 birds at 31 yards, he asked for a division, notwithstanding he had bet me $50 he would shoot me out. The same year I shot two days at Decatur, three days at Jacksonville, two days at Peoria and two days at Winona without a miss – a run of 735 straight, mostly at glass balls. Shortly after I defeated J. Frank Kleintz of Philadelphia, then the crack pigeon shot of the East, in a match at 100 live pigeons, score 88 to 84. Daniel W. Vorhees of Peoria backed me in this match, which was for one thousand dollars. We both used 10-gauge guns, trap and handle, and Kleintz gave me the hardest birds.

Novel Duck Shooting Before Large Audience

After shooting on the Sangamon until the ducks had mostly gone north, we broke camp and came home up the river. Doty lived at Henry, a town about 40 miles north of Peoria, while Wilky went home to Chillicothe.

On arriving in Peoria, I found Peoria Lake, which is a widening of the Illinois River for 18 miles, covered with bluebills, which were feeding on spill slops which were dumped in the lake from a glucose factory located on the shore only a few blocks above the foot of Main Street at the river front. The ducks would come within a hundred yards of the bank, fill up on this waste or slop, then leave and make room for others. The river was high and the lake had a strong current running south. It looked to me like one more chance for a big day's shoot.

21. *"The Hunting Season" at Bellvue, Iowa, circa 1920. Apparently, wives of the era were far more tolerant when their husbands brought game into the home for photography, especially when they nailed ducks and geese against the door.*

22. *These Iowa hunters of about 1900 travelled by buckboard to the marshes for this astounding bag of mallards and pintails.*

"THE HUNTING SEASON" AT BELLEVUE IA.

21

22

23

24

I hired a wide, flat-bottomed boat, towed it across the lake among the willows and cut a big boatload. Then I towed it back to the Peoria side and fixed up a brush battery covering the boat and building a blind to shoot from. In the morning at daylight I had the battery anchored at 100 yards from shore, with about 50 decoys set out to the east. I had sold my double gun and had only the old, despised, single-barrel muzzle-loader.

The bluebills commenced coming at daylight and I started shooting. A boy was stationed a few hundred yards below with a boat to pick up the ducks as they would float down. The day was bright and still, the water as smooth as glass, and the shooting the easiest I ever had in my life. The ducks would come to the decoys and when within about 40 yards I would rise up in my blind and they would start to climb, either to the left or right. I could take all the time needed and fill a duck full of No. 4 shot. I made one run of 57 straight without missing, being one of my longest straight runs on ducks.

Peoria was then a city of about 25,000 people, and soon spectators began to collect on the shore until the bank was lined with people watching me shoot, many of whom probably had never seen birds of any kind shot in the air before. My father was among the crowd. We lived only a short distance from the shore, and at noon he brought a dinner pail with a hot oyster stew and had it sent out to me. To eat a hot oyster stew out of a duck blind in the presence of a large, refined and appreciative audience was something new in the duck shooting line. I was the whole show and was surely "it." Later I shot in great crowds at tournaments; have shot individual matches before large numbers of people; have given skating exhibitions, played banjo solos, violin and French accordion solos before large audiences; played checkers against state champions and won, but never was the whole show either before or since.

My boatman picked up 156 bluebills that day, and others in boats picked up quite a lot while the picking was good. It was estimated that 200 ducks were killed that day by the old one-barrel gun. Most of the people who saw my shooting that day have passed on, but I am still alive at 86 years of age and able to shoot pretty well yet. I shot a couple of days a few years ago at one of the large ducking clubs in Southern California and the members were surprised. They said my shooting was a revelation to them. I did a little trap shooting also and several times got nearly 100 straight.

Many branches of sport such as golf, baseball, lawn tennis and others allow of large galleries of spectators, but this is the only time I have ever known of a large concourse of people watch a man shoot ducks.

Among the Geese and Sand Hill Cranes in North Dakota

My Parker No. 10 double gun handled large shot well, putting its charge of No. 1 or No. 2 shot into a 30-inch circle at 40 yards.

I had heard much about the goose shooting in North Dakota, so I took a trip up there. I stopped with a farmer 12 miles north of Dawson, North Dakota. A colony of New York farmers had taken up a tract of land just south of the Manitoba line, and had planted it all in wheat. It was called New York settlement and my stopping place was the nearest house to the railroad. All the other farmers had to pass the house in going to or from town.

This large tract of wheat was the first in the line of flight of the geese and cranes on their way south and it was a great feeding ground. I stopped with a farmer named Stinchcomb and W.B. Mershon knew him.

Here was a good opportunity to try out my Parker on long-range shooting and I took advantage of it. I used No. 1 shot. One afternoon, shooting from a pit in a stubble field, between 3 o'clock and sundown, I killed 46 Canada geese and 37 sand hill cranes. Five of the largest geese weighed 16-1/2 pounds each, while the lot would average around 11 pounds. The cranes ran about 6-1/2 pounds each. The total weight of the game shot inside of three hours was over 700 pounds. It filled our wagon box.

I could kill both geese and cranes up to 65 yards and had no trouble in killing pairs up to 60 yards when straight overhead.

Both the old Parker gun and myself decided it was time to go home after putting in a solid month with the geese and cranes. When we arrived at Dawson on the railroad I found that reports had been brought in from day to day by the farmers and to hear them tell it, a goose couldn't fly high enough to get out of reach of that old gun. What it had done to the geese and cranes was the talk of the town. The farmers were supplied first and the game not used by them was shipped to Minneapolis and Chicago. The trip had been successful in every way. In fact, as fine a trip as I ever had in all my career and one never to be forgotten.

from SUPREME DUCK SHOOTING STORIES, 1936

---

23. Minnesota's famed Heron Lake was a the scene of glorious duck shooting for sport hunters as well as commercial gunners. Here, in this 1887 photograph, a hunter retrieves a canvasback.

24. Wisconsin's heralded Horicon Marsh was the shooting grounds for, among other private hunt clubs, the Diana Shooting Club, whose members here show off their skiffs, circa 1900.

25

DUCK SHOOTING ON CLUB-FOOT LAKE ~ REELFOOT

Ah, whence dost thou come, O bird of widespread wing?
From what remotest shore does thou wondrous tidings bring?
Now, wither dost thou tend? Perchance to Southern clime,
Where calm lagoons are girdled in with orange and lime.
— Isaac McLellan

Up to the present time, duck shooting on Reelfoot has been attendant with risk – not for the ducks so much as for the shooters. Certain lawless elements have commanded this region so long that unless a "port" possesses the open sesame to the exclusive order of the P.C. – Pusher's Conference – of Hotel Samberg, it is an even draw as to whether he ought to venture upon these shores.

Jim Commons, Fatty Brooks, Slim Griffith, and sundry other pushers less famous, may punctuate the morning air with revolver shots which mean: "Get up, you lazy sports if you expect to get ducks today" or the signal may shout: "Look out, boys! New sport on the lake. May be a revenuer!" Or a particulary rapid staccato may scream: "Game warden!"

Claude, Jim and I did not fear the familiar perils of this watery wilderness for we were already initiated.

25. Three South Dakota goose hunters and their straining meat pole, circa 1905.

26. As long as men have hunted geese, they have had to pluck geese. This circa 1900 hunter is saving the down, ostensibly for mattress, pillow or quilt ticking.

27. Hunters of the Nebraska Sandhills ham it up for a portrait outside a sod house, circa 1912.

And, too, we recognized the fact that if it were not for the pusher's patent oar which enables him to pull facing the bow, we might now be resting at the bottom of the lake, strangled in the submarine forest of trapanatans or the twisted roots of the cypress.

In the year 1812 Nature coughed, gulped mightily and a slew-footed lake two hundred square miles in extent was born in the twinkling of an eye where nothing had been but peaceful landscape in the northwestern corner of Tennessee. The basin thus created was not filled with the waters of the muddy Mississippi, for its waters are crystal.

The P.C. decided that the forming of the lake caused the earthquake! We shooters could not dispute it. We could not swear that the lake, entire, had not existed before – sub-terra – and that by mixing its own waters with the subterranean fire had not belched itself bodily from the bowels of the earth. Nature has an effective

26

27

28. *An Iowa duck hunting camp of about 1916.*

29. *Not all duck hunting trips of the "glory years" resulted in large bags. This 1890 photo shows an East Coast hunter and his dog returning with only a drake wood duck and a drake blue-winged teal. Note, however, the teal's breeding plumage. These birds were shot on a spring hunt*

way of getting rid of her unpleasant in'ards very quickly, just as Claude does when he eats too much of Mrs. Smith's delightful cooking – which is nearly every time we go there.

At any rate, this weird stretch of water is a vast cemetery of trees. Everywhere their stumps and ragged skeletons stand stark monuments of a primeval forest. Some protrude from the depths like the sunken masts of a lost armada; others like the peaceful spiles of Venice; still other veterans like the banished admirals of an inland navy. The owls and heavy-winged "water-buzzards" have never left it, for here they find riotous subsistence upon the teeming fish. So do the furtive fishermen, not yet quite sure of their rights, though in times past they have fought – even murdered – for them in face of crooked legislation.

Our progressive pushers – Fatty and Jim – use live, trained decoys – "Dicks and Susies." These little feathered, intelligent friends trod familiarly over our legs with their pink, web feet, chattering with much joyous anticipation of the hunt as they clambered into our boats. Our guides had turned them out of their pens before daylight to "limber up." They are rarely ever fed; only when hunting is dull. We hunters had already eaten generously of Mrs. Smith's baked croppy (sic) fish, roast duck, fried coot, hot rolls, etc. Duck and man seemed ready for the fray.

Sam Applewhite's motor, after doing stunts over submerged log and snag, chugged us out beyond the pale of film ice and within reach of the sport. We soon ensconced ourselves in the curious blinds of Rat Island; the waist-high hollow stumps concealed among the curiously distorted boles and roots of the clumps of water cypress.

Our excited Dicks and Susies were soon turned loose to feed. There were only a few coots in sight. Fatty possessed one of those inimitable duck calls for which Reelfoot is famous and when his industrious decoys did not tune up with the proper duck chatter Fatty soliloquized in wild celery talk and umbrella nut conversation.

Very soon, with the help or our "pitching" Dicks and Susies, he pulled them down right out of the sky. Here they come! Our chilled veins and limbs were suddenly warmed with action. As the birds breasted against the wind to settle, we raised from our tree-clumps and let them have it.

Our decoys kept a comical eye heavenward and dodged our kill as it splashed into the half frozen waters of the lake. Down we went again. More nutty talk by Fatty, and here they came. Up we went like Jacks in boxes. Down came our feathered shower, the lifeless bodies often skidding for many feet across the firmer ice from the momentum of the fliers. We shot until our guns were too hot to hold comfortably, then we had lunch.

Unfortunately, that afternoon a great raft of coots a mile long settled off to our right; as a result the new ducks swerved off to their feeding grounds, though decoyed by us. This continued until we were compelled to bring in our faithful decoys and depart for Cane

30. The era of the double barrel: members of the Waupun (Wisconsin) Hunters Club pose proudly with their scatterguns.

Island. Although we shot among the coots frequently we could not disperse them. After our second round at Cane Island we reached our limit. There was a furtive exchange of glances in which temptation was written.

"Well," said Fatty, "we'll be going!" That settled it. It is an inviolable rule of the P.C. never to exceed the limit nor to shoot on the grounds before sunrise or after sunset. We obeyed the mandate by paddling our way homeward.

The next morning we were upon the water early. The ice was so thick it had to be broken in the "blow-holes" to allow the staking of the decoys. Presently Dicks and Susies were working bravely. Up came great clouds of redheads, mallards, teals, and a few canvasbacks. We let them have it at close range. After desultory shooting we were compelled to decamp to Goose Basin on account of the changing wind. We did not go for geese, however, for these fair creatures did not deign to descend from the Flying Wedge – the Aerial Goose Limited, "no stop-overs." They skimmed by a mile high like a whizzing arrow winging southward.

Fatty chattered some more cunning duck talk while we battered them from the reeds. Our boatload of game at close of day spoke eloquently of our success. Jim picked up a lost "Dick" as we turned to go. He was quacking desolately in a lonesome pool. His stay with us was very brief, however. The welcome he received from his feathered brethren was not to his taste, so he put over the gunwale and dived into the depths of Reelfoot. He never came up.

He may be now feeding on rich umbrella nut and wild celery in duck heaven or perhaps he went to a hotter place reserved for feathered Judases who betray their kind. He had evidently been guilty of some infraction of the laws of Dicks and Susies. We did not stay to inquire but threaded our way back to a good, hot supper and a more hospitable welcome than he received from his kind.

– by Robert Lindsay Mason,
in DUCK & GOOSE SHOOTING,
Easton Brothers Press, 1916

143